HOW

IN SIMI

PONTIFICAL FUNCTIONS

St. John Berchmans
Patron of Altar Boys
1599–1621

HOW TO SERVE
IN SIMPLE, SOLEMN, AND
PONTIFICAL FUNCTIONS

Dom Matthew Britt, O.S.B.

ST. MARTIN'S ABBEY, LACEY, WASHINGTON

TAN Books
Charlotte, North Carolina

Imprimi Potest: Lambertus Burton, O.S.B.
                    Abbas S. Martini

Nihil Obstat: H. B. Ries
                    Censor librorum

Imprimatur: ☩ Samuel A. Stritch
                    Archiepiscopus Milwaukiensis
                    October 18, 1933

ISBN: 978-0-89555-888-6

Cover design by Milo Persic. The cover photo and photos for Figures 3, 4, 5, 6 and 10 were taken by Milo Persic at St. John Cantius Church, Chicago, IL, in cooperation with the Canons Regular of St. John Cantius and Fr. Scott Haynes, S.J.C.

Printed and bound in the United States of America.

TAN Books
Charlotte, North Carolina
www.TANBooks.com
2014

Introibo ad altare Dei.
  Ad Deum qui laetificat juventutem meam.

I will go unto the altar of God.
  To God, who giveth joy to my youth.

Contents

15. Vespers in the Presence of the
    Blessed Sacrament Exposed 136

16. Vespers for the Dead...................... 138

17. Benediction of the Blessed Sacrament
    with Servers Only 139

18. Manner of Serving a Low Mass
    Celebrated by a Dominican............... 144

    Reference List 147

    Index 149

Preface

AMONG THE FEW THINGS accomplished by the writer during the course of a somewhat busy but ill-spent life has been the preparation of three manuals or guides for servers, each of which has been independent of its predecessor. The first, a *Vade Mecum for Servers*, was published in 1895; the second, a *Ceremonial for Altar Boys*, appeared in 1898. Both of these were written several years before the author's ordination. The third booklet is now making its bow, and it is dedicated to the young men in our preparatory seminaries, with the hope that some day one of them may write a better book.

Since the earlier handbooks were published, and they were pioneers in the field, many changes have taken place that affect a work of this kind. Furthermore, many new and exhaustive ceremonials, written in a systematic and scientific manner, have appeared in Latin, English, French, and German. In the preparation of the present work extensive use has been made of such recent literature. Regarding Pontifical ceremonies, and Mass in particular, a special word must be said. The scholarly works of Stehle and Schober have been followed throughout. Each of these authors explains separately and concisely, but with sufficient detail, the duties of each minister in the sanctuary, both sacred and inferior.

It is not claimed that the method of serving as set forth in this manual is, in every case, the only correct one. Anyone who is familiar with more than one book on the subject need not be told this. The rubrics provide a fair outline of the servers' duties; liturgical writers supply the details. The rubrics are often quite general, and at times none too clear. As a result they are not always interpreted in the same way. Custom, too, plays its part, even where there is no ambiguity in the law. From these and from similar sources arise the differences that are found in approved authors. Any approved author may be safely followed.

It need scarcely be said, and the fact is here stressed, that the present work contains considerable matter and many references that are not intended for the servers but for those who instruct them or provide for their needs in the sanctuary. This is especially true of some of the sections included under "Common Ceremonial Actions." Thus, to mention only two, the section on Vesture will be of interest to the members of the altar society, if it be their duty to provide appropriate garments for the servers. Nor is any apology required for the much-needed section on the little silvery-toned Altar Bell which is being so generally replaced by a variety of unrubrical, clangorous instruments that distract the recollected and make the angels weep.

The author expresses his grateful appreciation to his confrere, Dom Raphael Heider, O.S.B., for the cover design and for the twenty-eight drawings and other illustrations that were made by him especially for this book. Acknowledgment must also be made to the Rev. Vincent A. McCormick, S.J., of Woodstock College, for the frontispiece, an unusual picture of St. John Berchmans, the patron saint of altar boys.

For information concerning the St. John Berchmans' Sanctuary Society, its origin, rules, indulgences, etc., see the *Manual of the St. John Berchmans' Sanctuary Society* published by the Apostleship of Prayer (1927).

The author will be deeply grateful to anyone who will point out anything in the present work that is contrary to either the letter or the spirit of the rubrics. However, this implies no request for the reader's preference in matters that are variously interpreted by approved authors.

PREFACE TO THIRD EDITION

The present edition contains only minor changes, which were made for the sake of clearness. Section 34, on page 35, is new; the one on Mass pictures has been deleted since the pictures, published abroad, are no longer obtainable. A work of great value on the rubrics has just been published. Its author, the Rev. J. B. O'Connell, is the editor and reviser of Fortescue's *The Roman Rite*. The work is an exhaustive one in three volumes on *The Celebration of Mass* (Bruce, Milwaukee, 1941). It compares favorably with such standard works as Bishop Van der Stappen's *Sacra Liturgia*. It is a storehouse of rubrical knowledge for priests, seminarians, masters of ceremonies, and others.

Key to Symbols

Bishop.

Celebrant wearing a chasuble.

Celebrant wearing a cope.

Deacon.

Subdeacon.

Master of ceremonies.

Thurifer with censer

Thurifer without censer.

Cross-bearer whether subdeacon or server.

First acolyte.

Second acolyte.

Torch-bearer.

Assistant in cope.

Assistant priest.

Assistant deacon.

Crozier-bearer.

Miter-bearer.

Book-bearer.

Candle-bearer.

Server with holy water vessel.

Candlestick.

Acknowledgments

We wish to thank Fr. Scott Haynes, S.J.C. of the Canons Regular of St. John Cantius, St. John Cantius parish, Chicago, for facilitating the taking of the photographs which appear in this book (Figures 3, 4, 5, 6 and 10). For more information on the Canons Regular of St. John Cantius, please visit www.canons-regular.org. Thanks go also to Milo Persic, the photographer, as well as to the servers who participated.

—TAN Books and Publishers

HOW TO SERVE
IN SIMPLE, SOLEMN, AND
PONTIFICAL FUNCTIONS

Chapter 1
Common Ceremonial Actions

THE MATTERS TREATED under Common Ceremonial Actions are of very great importance. They are the fundamentals of all good serving. Collectively they comprise the chief rules of conduct which Holy Church prescribes for those who minister before the Eucharistic King. Without a knowledge of them no altar boy can edify others by his presence in the sanctuary. What he is here taught will be helpful to him whether he remains a layman or becomes a priest. In the latter event he will have nothing to unlearn in the days of his priestly ministry.

1. Conduct

An altar boy enjoys a distinct privilege in being allowed to serve at the altar. Every server is a page in God's house. This being the case, his conduct must be above reproach. In the sanctuary he must be reverent, thoughtful, and attentive. Nor will he ever be an occasion of distraction, much less of scandal, to others. A lack of reverence for sacred things is one of the great sins of the age. Unfortunately, at times it finds its way into the sanctuary, where by contrast it becomes extremely conspicuous.

2. Cleanliness

No altar boy with a sense of self-respect would enter the home of a friend knowing that his face and hands are

1

dirty, his hair uncombed, and his shoes unpolished. Nor will the same boy neglect these proprieties when he enters the house of his dearest Friend, the sanctuary of the Living God.

An altar boy should be scrupulously neat and clean. And this cleanliness should extend not only to his own person but to everything in the sacristy and in the sanctuary. Special attention should be paid to cassock and surplice, the censer, charcoal, match stubs, candlesticks, and to the lighting of candles on the altar.

3. Attention

The server should pay strict attention to the Mass he is serving, and no attention whatever to anything else that is going on in the church, not even to a Solemn High Mass that is being celebrated at another altar. This applies even to such parts of another Mass as the Elevation or the Communion of the faithful.

Attention also implies that the server unite himself in thought and action as closely as possible to the priest whose Mass he is serving. When the priest makes the sign of the cross on himself during the prayers at the foot of the altar, at the Introit, at the end of the *Gloria* and *Credo,* at the beginning of each Gospel, and after the *Sanctus,* the server also signs himself. Nor should he neglect to bow his head when he hears the Holy Name of Jesus read or sung. The degree to which this union with the priest can be carried depends upon the age of the server and the amount of instruction he receives. With young servers these matters should not be too greatly stressed.

4. Vesture

The proper dress for any server is a black cassock and a plain linen surplice.

a) The Cassock.   While there is no rubric forbidding the use of red cassocks, their use violates the spirit of the liturgy as does the use of cinctures, birettas, and the vesting of altar boys as miniature prelates. The sanctuary is not a stage.[1]

b) Putting on the Cassock. In putting on the cassock the server first puts his right arm into the right sleeve, then his left arm into the other sleeve. Then, and this is most important, he buttons all the buttons, not merely a part of them. It need hardly be said that the cassock should fit the server, that it should be neither too long nor too short. Nor should it be torn, wrinkled, wanting in buttons, or spattered with wax.

c) The Surplice. There are certain kinds of surplices that are not in keeping with the spirit of the liturgy. Among these are the lace surplice, the pleated surplice, and the short surplice of whatever material it may be made. No altar boy is more becomingly vested than one who has on a simple, long, linen surplice, immaculately clean. Moreover, it is preferable that it should have a wide opening at the neck where the fabric is neatly gathered. It is immaterial whether the opening be square or circular in shape. The surplice should have no slit down the front, no ribbons, strings, hooks, or buttons.[2]

---

1. "Cassocks of altar boys should be black. It is fitting that a boy serving Mass should wear the clerical garb, which consists, for all clerics who are not prelates, of a black cassock and a white surplice." *Amer. Eccl. Review,* Dec., 1932, p. 644.

   "The common dress for all servers," says Fortescue, "and for all who assist at any function in choir is a black cassock and a white linen surplice." *The Roman Rite,* p. 11.

   "The use of red for such cassocks and accessories," says Dom Roulin, "dates from the nineteenth century and no earlier, and however attractive red cassocks may be to some, and distracting to others, they do not really harmonize well with the dignity of Christian worship. As ministers of the altar the servers have dignity enough from their office without these red vestments; and I believe that both for them and for choir-boys the true and proper vestments are the black cassock and the full surplice." *Vestments and Vesture,* p. vi.

2. "It is astonishing," says Fortescue, "how modern the little cotta (surplice) to the waist is. Illustrations of . . . the eighteenth century still show long full surplices without lace; and France and Germany have never brought the surplice above the knee. I need hardly point out that artistically the beauty and dignity of this garment are entirely a matter of long full folds. A long surplice falling in folds, with wide sleeves — one, in short, made according to St. Charles's rules — is an exceedingly handsome garment." *Vestments of the Roman Rite,* p. 110. See especially Dom Roulin's *Vestments and Vesture* (Herder), pp. 29–35. In it will be found a good account of the surplice and several illustrations of both correct and incorrect models. Every ladies' altar society should have a copy of this book.

d) Putting on the Surplice. To put on the surplice properly, the server holds it with one hand at the top, and with the other he opens it from below. Then placing both hands in the opening he passes it over his head and onto his shoulders. He then puts his right arm into the right sleeve, and his left arm into the other. He carefully adjusts the garment so that it will hang properly about his person.

In taking off the surplice, the server withdraws his left arm from its sleeve; then, lifting the left side of the surplice over his head, he withdraws his right arm. In putting on or removing the surplice haste should be avoided.

5. The Sign of the Cross

To make the sign of the cross properly, the server holds his left hand open and extended against his breast. It is held a little below the breast, but not too low. Then with the right hand also extended, with the fingers joined and the palm facing the server, he touches with the tips of the fingers his forehead, breast, left shoulder, and lastly his right shoulder. The lines of the cross should be traced fully and deliberately, not hurriedly and thoughtlessly. The rubrics prescribe a generous-sized cross, not a niggardly one.

If the words accompany the sign, they are distributed thus: At the words *In nomine Patris* he touches his forehead; at *Filii* his breast just above his left hand; and while passing the hand from the left to the right shoulder he says *et Spiritus Sancti.* Joining his hands, he says *Amen.*

At the beginning of each Gospel the server makes three small signs of the cross on his forehead, lips, and breast. The left hand is held as above. The right is extended with the palm facing the server. Then with the soft part of the thumb, not with the nail, he makes the triple sign on his forehead, lips, and breast. The third is made above, not below, the left hand.

6. Genuflections

There are two kinds of genuflections, simple and double. A simple genuflection is made by touching the floor with the right knee near the left heel. The hands are kept joined before the breast. They must never rest upon the knee nor upon any other object. No bow of any kind is made. This genuflection must not be prolonged; the knee must not remain resting on the floor. In making this genuflection, either too great haste or too great slowness is equally improper.

A double genuflection is made by kneeling on both knees and making a moderate bow. This bow is explained in the following Section.

There is an important decree[3] concerning genuflections that are to be made before an altar on which the Blessed Sacrament is not reserved. It applies to servers in all Masses whether they be read or sung.

The following quotation contains a translation of the decree and an opinion regarding its application to us. "The decree of Nov. 23, 1906, is the only rule to be observed now, even in this country. Therefore 'the minister serving Mass at the altar on which the Blessed Sacrament is not reserved, should genuflect on one knee on arriving at the altar, as often as he passes before the middle of the altar, and on retiring from the altar.' "[4]

7. Bows or Inclinations

There are three kinds of bows, which may be conveniently designated by their abbreviations. Thus bow P stands for profound bow; bow M for moderate bow; and bow H for simple bow, which is a bow of the head only.

a) The Profound Bow, Bow P. This bow is made by bending the head and body so low that if the hands were extended it would be possible to touch the knees with the

---

3. S.R.C. 4193, 1, Nov. 23, 1906.
4. *Amer. Eccl. Review,* Dec., 1932, p. 643.

tips of the fingers. As this bow is made only while standing, there is no instance, not even during the *Confiteor,*
when an altar boy makes it.[5]

b) The Moderate Bow, Bow M. This is marked
inclination of the head and shoulders, but as the name
implies, it is less low than the preceding bow. This is the
bow that a kneeling person makes while reciting the
Confiteor. One who is standing makes a profound bow.

c) The Simple Bow, Bow H. This is made by bending the head only. By some this bow is subdivided into
profound, medium, and slight. Unless otherwise specified,
the term *bow H,* throughout this book, signifies a profound bow of the head. It is very common. It is the proper
salutation to make to the cross in the sacristy, to the choir
or clergy, to the celebrant, and before and after incensing
anyone.

8. Bows to the Choir or Clergy

Since most altar boys have no idea of what is meant
by the term *choir* as used in the rules given below, a
brief explanation of it will not be out of place. In some
churches, where there are a number of clergy, as in reli-
gious communities, the members occupy seats or stalls
either in the sanctuary or near the sanctuary. These
stalls are arranged so that the occupants face one
another, one half being at the Gospel side, the other
half at the Epistle side. Theoretically these should do
all the singing that is to be done; practically, however,
they may do only some of it, or none at all. For ceremonial purposes the terms *choir* and *clergy* may be
regarded as synonymous. The term *choir* in no sense
refers to the body of singers that occupies the gallery
above the front entrance to the church. No attention is
to be paid to them.

---

5. S.R.C. 4179, 1. See Callewaert, p. 30; Wapelhorst, 97, 5; 131, 4; Fortescue, p. 24.

If there is a liturgical choir present, the servers bow to it as indicated in the rules given below. The purpose of rules *a* and *b* is to make clear which should come first, the bows to the choir or the genuflection to the altar. Rules *c* and *d* state which side of the choir one should bow to first, the Gospel side or the Epistle side. By *function* is meant Mass, Vespers, etc.

a) On entering the sanctuary at the beginning of any function, if the celebrant and servers have to pass through the choir before reaching the altar, they bow to the clergy at the entrance of the stalls and genuflect before the altar when they reach it.[6]

b) But if they do not have to pass through the choir in order to reach the altar, as is the case in most of our American churches, they first genuflect before the altar and then bow to the choir or clergy.[7]

c) At the beginning, and at the end, of any function a bow is made first to those at the Gospel side, and then to those at the Epistle side. But if, by any chance, the greater dignitary should be at the Epistle side, a bow is made first to that side.

d) During any function, as before the singing of the Epistle and Gospel in Solemn High Mass, and after the *Aperi Domine* in Vespers, a bow is made first to the side of the choir from which one turns or departs, and secondly to the side toward which one is to go. No regard is paid to "the side of greater dignity."[8] The rule has many applications.

e) Whenever the thurifer, either alone or with the torch-bearers, enters or leaves the sanctuary during any function, he first genuflects before the altar, and then bows to the choir or clergy.

---

6. *Caer. Ep.* XVII, 1.
7. *Caer. Ep.* XXX, 1. The directions given in most of our ceremonials regarding rules *a* and *b* above are, to say the least, misleading. The misunderstanding arises from the two contradictory directions given in Chapters XVII and XXX of the *Caeremoniale Episcoporum*. The solution given above is taken from the *Ephemerides Liturgicae*, XIV, 1900, p. 369, which solution is repeatedly referred to by Van der Stappen. The term rendered "pass through" above, may also be rendered simply "pass" or "pass by," owing to the different places a choir may occupy. See the article on "Choir" in the *Catholic Encyclopedia*.
8. *Caer. Ep.* Lib. I, XVIII, 13; Fortescue, p. 216; Callewaert, p. 23.

f) While the Blessed Sacrament is exposed, no bows are made to the choir or to anyone else, regardless of his rank or dignity.[9]

g) No bows are made to anyone from the Consecration till Communion in any Mass.

h) When the bishop of the diocese is present in the sanctuary, a bow is made to him, but no bows are made to the choir.[10]

9. Postures of the Body

Under this heading are treated such things as enter into a server's general deportment in the sanctuary. When a server does not observe them it is probably an indication that in his training the following rules have not been sufficiently stressed. In such matters, however, extremes must be avoided. It is equally improper for a server to be careless and slovenly in what he does, or for him to be ridiculously stilted and artificial in his actions.[11]

a) Standing. When standing the server always faces the altar when he can do so without violating any other rule. He stands naturally and with his hands folded, with his head erect, and with his eyes directed toward the altar or modestly cast down. He genuflects whenever the priest does. Any exception to this rule will be found in the proper place.

b) Kneeling. The server kneels facing the altar. His hands are joined unless he is holding a book. He should kneel as quietly and as motionless as possible and pay close attention to what is going on at the altar. He should especially avoid looking about him or behind him. The latter is sometimes done by servers who make a great fuss

---

9. S.R.C. 2544; 2928, 6.
10. Callewaert, p. 23.
11. See Martinucci-Menghini, II, pp. 550–551; and Fortescue, p. 35.

about covering their feet with their cassock. It is much more unbecoming for a server to look behind him than it is to kneel with uncovered feet.

c) Sitting. While seated he sits erect with his hands resting palms downward on his knees. The knees should be kept close together. The feet must never be crossed. In changing from a sitting to a kneeling position, or from a kneeling to a sitting position, he first stands erect momentarily, and then kneels or sits as the case may be. This rule is frequently violated, and something akin to slouchiness results.

d) Walking. There is nothing in a server's general conduct more noticeable than his manner of walking. Here again extremes must be avoided. Hasty walking, and unduly slow walking are alike objectionable. Long strides and short mincing steps are equally out of place in the sanctuary. It is important that a server should hold his head and body erect, and that they should not sway from side to side with his steps. Nor should a server ever attempt to genuflect while walking. Before genuflecting he should first come to a full stop, and stand directly facing the altar. He should never walk backwards or sideways either on the floor or on the steps of the altar, but should first turn fully in the direction in which he is to go.

When two servers are walking together they walk side by side, unless the way is narrow. If the way is narrow, the second, the one at the left, precedes the first. It is never permissible for one server to walk only partly in front of another.

e) The Eyes. The eyes are troublesome members. A good server will guard them with care. They should be either modestly cast down or directed toward the altar. They should never be permitted to wander about the sanctuary nor even beyond the communion rail into the body of the church. Such behavior shows both a want of attention and a very great lack of self-control.

f) The Hands. When a server is standing or kneeling, his hands, if not otherwise occupied, are joined palm to palm with the right thumb over the left in the form of a cross. The elbows rest naturally against the sides. The hands, when joined, point upward at an angle of about forty-five degrees.[12] It is equally incorrect to hold the hands upward against the breast, or to hold them so low that they are parallel with the floor. The hands, whether one or both, must never be permitted to hang down at the server's sides.

g) The Feet. A server whether kneeling or sitting should never cross his feet. While kneeling, if it be difficult to hold the feet erect and parallel, the heels at least should be kept together.

h) Striking the Breast. The breast is struck with the right hand, which is held half open and not clenched in the form of a fist. The server does not strike his breast during the priest's *Confiteor,* nor at the *Nobis quoque peccatoribus,* nor at the *Domine non sum dignus.*[13] The only time that he strikes his breast at the *Domine non sum dignus* is when it is said just before he himself receives Holy Communion.[14] The words, which mean "Lord I am not worthy," apply then to himself. When the priest says them in the Mass, or before giving Communion to the faithful, they apply to the priest or to the faithful, as the case may be.

Servers must not fall into the habit of striking their breasts whenever any word or phrase is repeated three times. Some even carry this so far that they strike their breasts at the words: "O clement, O loving, O sweet Virgin Mary!"

i) Uniformity of Action. Too great stress cannot be laid on this rule. When two or more servers are to perform any action in common, such as to genuflect, bow, kneel,

---

12. Van der Stappen, V, p. 3; Wapelhorst, 100.
13. S.R.C. 3535, 3.
14. Van der Stappen, Vol. V, p. 47; Menghini, p. 44.

sit, or rise, it must be done at one and the same moment, and in exactly the same manner. This uniformity is obtained only by drilling or rehearsal. In the making of a well-trained group of servers, books have their place, and oral instruction has its place, but without frequent and careful drilling both of them combined will not produce the desired results.

In the timing of an action the second server, the one at the left, should be guided by the first. When several servers are to perform an action in common, one of them should give a signal loud enough to be heard by all.

10. Lighting and Extinguishing Candles

a) **One Row of Candles.** The candles at the Epistle side are lit first,[15] beginning with the one nearest the cross. Then those at the Gospel side are lit in the same manner. They are extinguished in the reverse order. See Figure 1. Rule: In lighting, count forward; in extinguishing, count backward.

b) **Two or More Rows of Candles.** When two or more rows of candles are to be lit, the server first lights

Fig. 1. How to light one row of candles.

15. S.R.C. 4198, 9.

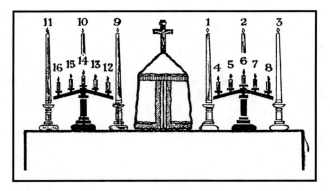

Fig. 2. How to light more than one row of candles.

all the candles at the Epistle side, then those at the Gospel side. He first lights the top row at the Epistle side, beginning with the candle that is nearest the cross. He lights the second row in the same order, and the third, if there be one. He then lights the candles on the Gospel side in the same manner. The candles are extinguished in the reverse order. See Figure 2.

The decree referred to above seems to imply that one server is to light all the candles. But if two servers light them, each lights the candles on one side,[16] beginning with the one nearest the cross in the top row. They extinguish them in the reverse order.

c) How to Use Candle Lighter and Extinguisher. In lighting candles the taper should be held upward so that it will give forth only a small flame. A small flame will light a candle as quickly as a large one. If the taper is held downward, it will give forth a large flame which may not only cause drops of wax to fall on the altar, but by heating the end of the lighter it may clog it up with molten wax.

In extinguishing candles it is neither necessary nor advisable that the extinguisher be pressed down on the candle, or that it even touch it. If it does, it is apt to

---

16. Fortescue, pp. 100 and 103.

Fig. 3. How the censer is carried when it does not contain incense.

become partly filled with wax which the candle flames will cause to drip on the altar.

In either lighting or extinguishing candles let the server, above all things, be neat, and let him go about his task with a quiet dignity. It is a pleasure to watch a well-trained server light or extinguish candles. It is an art, and in many places a lost art, owing to the hurry, want of method, and carelessness of the one who lights them.

11. The Censer, How Carried

General Rule. When the censer does not contain incense it is carried with the left hand; but after incense has been put in, it is carried with the right. The incense boat is held against the breast in the unoccupied hand.

a) **Without Incense.** When the censer does not contain incense it is carried by gripping the chains with the left hand just below the cap or disk at the top. The cover of the censer is raised slightly to permit better ventilation to the charcoal, but the censer is not swung to and fro. See Figure 3.

b) **With Incense.** After incense has been put in, the censer may be carried as described in the preceding paragraph, but with the right hand. On more formal occasions, however, as when the thurifer walks at the head of a procession, or when he goes to the place where the Gospel is to be sung, he employs the following method: He passes his thumb through the ring at the top of the disk, and thus supports the weight of the censer. He puts his middle finger through the other ring which enables him to raise or lower the cover of the censer. Or, if he prefers, he may reverse the position of his thumb and finger in the two rings. See Figure 4. While the censer contains incense, the thurifer gently swings it to and fro, but this should not cause any swaying motion of his body.[17]

While kneeling or genuflecting, the thurifer holds the censer with one hand at the top; with the other he grasps the chains near the middle.

12. Putting Incense into the Censer

When the thurifer brings the censer to the celebrant he hands the boat to the person who is standing at the celebrant's right, whether it be the deacon, the master of ceremonies, or an acolyte. He then takes hold of the chains with his left hand just below the disk, and with his right he draws up the cover about four inches. He brings his left hand to his breast, and with his right he holds the censer at a convenient height for the priest to put incense into it.

Fig. 4. How the censer is carried when it contains incense.

See Figure 5. After the incense has been blessed, and not before, he closes and lowers the censer. It is important that the thurifer should remember that incense is always blessed except during Benediction and at other times when the Blessed Sacrament alone is to be incensed.

13. Presenting the Censer

Two cases are possible: (a) When the censer is given to someone who is not to use it himself. In this case the thurifer holds the chains at the top with his right hand,

---

17. The rule for carrying the censer is given in the *Caer. Ep.* I, XI, 7, but authorities differ in its interpretation. See Callewaert, pp. 53–54.

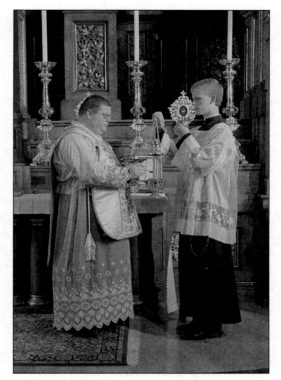

Fig. 5. How the censer is held while
incense is being put into it. Illustration
shows positions of priest and thurifer
only: see Fig. 16, p. 76.

and thus presents it to the deacon or to the master of
ceremonies, who in turn hands it to the celebrant or to
the person who is to use it. (b) But when the thurifer
gives the censer directly to the celebrant or to the minister who is to use it, he holds the chains with both
hands. The right hand grips the top of the chains just
under the disk, and the left, the lower part. The upper
part is then placed in the celebrant's left hand, and the
lower in his right. In both cases haste should be avoided,
and the thurifer's actions should be slow, graceful, and

dignified. To handle the censer gracefully requires careful drilling and no little practice.

14. How to Incense

The easiest way to learn how to incense a person or an object is by watching someone do it who does it accurately and gracefully. The act of incensing is in no way complicated, but it is one which requires many words to explain.

To handle the censer properly the thurifer takes the top of the chains in his left hand and holds it against his breast. With his right hand he takes hold of the chains a short distance above the cover, passing them between the first and second fingers. The three remaining fingers are held together under the chains to aid in swinging the censer toward the person to be incensed. A profound bow of the head is made both before and after incensing anyone. This bow is made also by the one who is being incensed. While a server is being incensed he should face the person who is incensing him, bowing before and after.

There are two kinds of incensing, one of which consists of a single swing of the censer toward the person incensed, the other of a double swing.

a) Single Swing. To incense with a single swing the thurifer raises the censer to the level of his breast, and at the same time he swings the censer out toward the person he is incensing. He then lets it fall to about the level of his knees. This act is repeated according to the number of swings that are to be given.

b) Double Swing. To incense with a double swing the thurifer raises the censer to the level of his face, then swings it outward toward the person he is incensing; repeating this outward swing he then lowers the censer. This raising and twice-repeated swinging of the censer constitutes one double swing.

c) The celebrant in Mass and Vespers is incensed with three double swings; the deacon with two; the master of ceremonies with one; each acolyte with one. The people are incensed with three single swings,[18] one down the middle, the next toward the Epistle side, and the last toward the Gospel side. Additional information will be found in the proper place.

15. The Boat-Bearer

The duty of the boat-bearer, if there be one, is to carry the incense boat. The rubrics make no provision for such a server, but many of the best authorities mention him.[19] If there is a boat-bearer, there is no reason why he, and not the thurifer, should not present the boat to the deacon and receive it from him. Callewaert everywhere presumes that there is a boat-bearer and that he hands the boat to the deacon and not to the master of ceremonies. Where there is no boat-bearer, authorities are divided. Probably the better method is for the thurifer to hand the boat to the master of ceremonies, who in turn gives it to the deacon. Against this practice, however, one could quote Martinucci and Van der Stappen.

16. Presenting Objects

Whenever possible, objects are presented with the right hand and received with the same. When one hand is occupied the other is held open and extended against the breast.

17. Kissing Objects Presented to the Celebrant

Three different practices obtain, only one of which should be adopted and followed by all the servers in the same church.

---

18. Fortescue, p. 98; Callewaert, p. 202.
19. De Herdt, II, 15; *Baltimore Ceremonial,* p. 143; Geryanti-Merati, I, p. 107; Fortescue, pp. 95–96; Callewaert, 53.

a) A rubric and a decree of the Congregation of Rites direct the server to kiss both cruets at the Offertory.[20] Some authorities omit all reference to the kissing of any other objects by altar boys. Among these are our own *Baltimore Ceremonial* and Wapelhorst. "By custom these oscula (kisses) are frequently omitted altogether by laymen."[21] Outside of seminaries, preparatory and major, this custom has much to commend it.

b) Others direct the server, when presenting an object, to kiss first the object, and then the hand of the celebrant. But when receiving it, he is to kiss first the hand and then the object.[22] The reason for both rules is solely one of convenience.

c) Others again direct the server to kiss whatever object he gives to the celebrant or receives from him, but he is never to kiss the celebrant's hand.[23]

d) In Requiem Masses and in Masses said in presence of the Blessed Sacrament exposed, no objects, not even the cruets, are kissed. On the Feast of the Purification and on Palm Sunday, when receiving a candle or palm, the server first kisses the newly blessed candle or palm and then the hand of the celebrant.[24]

18. Presenting the Cruets

The cruets are held at the base, and the handles are turned toward the left, parallel with the end of the altar or the top step. Each cruet is presented with the right hand. This is true whether there is one server or two, as will be explained in the proper place. The server kisses each cruet, both before giving it to the priest, and on receiving it back.[25] This kiss is imparted by merely

---

20. *Ritus cel.* VII, 4; S.R.C. 4193, 2.
21. Fortescue, p. 82, and especially p. XXIII.
22. This is the rule given in the *Caer. Ep.* I, XVIII, 16. All authorities apply it to the deacon and subdeacon, and some extend it to the inferior ministers or servers. Fortescue, Martinucci, Menghini, Stehle, Schober, and others.
23. De Herdt, I, 299; Callewaert, pp. 44 and 158.
24. S.R.C. 2148, 5.
25. *Ritus celebrandi*, VII, 4; S.R.C. 4193, 2.

touching the handle or the middle of the cruet with the closed lips. They are not kissed in Requiem Masses nor in Masses said in the presence of the Blessed Sacrament exposed. Nor are they kissed in Solemn High Mass, because they are not presented directly to the celebrant but to the subdeacon. Nor are they kissed at the ablutions in any Mass.[26]

19. Care of the Cruets

Before filling a cruet it should be drained. If there is the slightest indication that it is not clean it should be thoroughly rinsed out and then drained. The cruets should not be filled to the top. The necks at least should be left empty. After filling a cruet, its foot or base should be wiped dry. A drop of wine or water falling on a starched altar cloth leaves an unsightly stain. After the *Lavabo* the cruets should not be placed on the wet dish but upon the credence table. If it is the server's duty to take care of the cruets after Mass, he should rinse out the wine cruet twice. Both should be drained and the stoppers put in them.

20. The Processional Cross

The processional cross, which is really a crucifix with a long staff, is carried at the head of the procession. The figure of our Lord on the cross faces in the direction in which the procession is moving. The cross-bearer is accompanied by two acolytes with lighted candles. These three never genuflect but merely bow their heads when others genuflect. In those processions in which the Blessed Sacrament is not carried the thurifer precedes the cross-bearer.[27]

An archbishop's cross is not carried at the head of the procession but immediately before the archbishop and

---

26. Fortescue, p. 87; Van der Stappen, V, p. 47; *Ephem. Lit.*, XI, 1897, p. 609.
27. Van der Stappen, V, pp. 32–35.

his assistants robed in their vestments. The figure on the archbishop's cross always faces the archbishop. In a procession of this kind if it be of some length, there may be two cross-bearers and two sets of acolytes. One cross would then head the procession, and the other would precede the archbishop.

21. Acolytes' Candlesticks

a) How Carried. When the two acolytes are standing or walking together, or when the subdeacon or cross-bearer is between them, it is prescribed that they hold their candlesticks in the following manner: The first acolyte, the one on the right, holds his candlestick just under the knob with his right hand, and he puts his left under its foot. The second holds his left hand under the knob, and places his right under the foot.[28] Care should be taken that they be held equally high and as nearly straight as possible. See Figure 6. It cannot be stated too strongly that at no time do the acolytes carry candlesticks with unlighted candles in them. There is no exception to this rule. During the singing of the Gospel in Solemn Requiem Masses, and on Holy Saturday and the Eve of Pentecost, the acolytes stand beside the subdeacon with their hands joined before their breast. Their lighted candles remain on the credence table. They stand thus also during the Gospel at the end of the Passion as often as it is sung.

b) Material and Structure. According to Bishop Van der Stappen, acolytes' candlesticks should be made of brass or silver and they should have a broad round base. They must have a knob midway between the top and the bottom. Regarding their height, he suggests that they be not less than sixteen inches for ordinary use, and thirty-two for greater feasts and for use in processions.[29]

---

28. *Caer. Ep.* Lib. I, XI, 8.
29. Vol. III, p. 117. Care should be taken to purchase only such acolytes' candlesticks as are both artistically beautiful and liturgically correct.

Fig. 6. How the acolytes should hold
their candlesticks.

22. Torch-Bearers: General Remarks

In any sung Mass and in Benediction there may be
from two to eight torch-bearers. The number should be
even. As eight is the greatest number allowed in a
Pontifical High Mass,[30] it may be inferred that a greater
number must never be employed in any function. At the
beginning of any service they enter the sanctuary
together walking two by two behind the acolytes. If they
differ in height, the shorter should precede. If they carry
torches, they hold them at the middle, and hold them

---

30. *Caer. Ep.* Lib. II, VIII, 68.

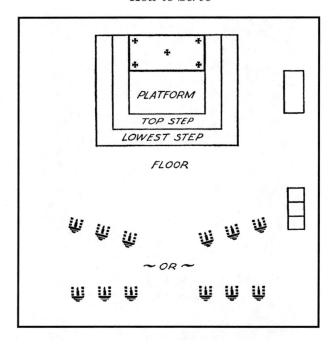

Fig. 7. The torch-bearers' place in the sanctuary:
how the altar steps are named in this book.

equally high. Those at the right carry their torches in
their right hand, those at the left in their left. The unoccupied hand is held open against the breast. After the
genuflection made in common they go to their places. The
places they occupy will depend on the shape and size of
the sanctuary. They usually form either a single row
directly in front of the altar, or two rows, one at each side
of the altar.

23. Unnecessary Servers

As to the number of servers that should take part in
any function, the rubrics are sufficiently explicit, and
where they are not, approved authors should be con-
sulted. There is a tendency in many churches to employ
a greater number of servers than are required. This is a

mistake. There is no beauty in mere numbers. "It does not add to the dignity of a rite that a crowd of useless boys stands about the sanctuary doing nothing.[31] "Too many servers may easily become a nuisance, nay, even a scandal to the people."[32]

Additional servers, raw recruits, are often placed in the sanctuary to be instructed in the ceremonies by older servers. This practice has nothing to commend it. Aside from the fact that very few altar boys are qualified to instruct others, there remains the additional impropriety of imparting such instruction during Mass or Benediction. Furthermore, this traditional or "handed-down" method of teaching the ceremonies is one of the chief causes of the slipshod serving which so often distracts or scandalizes devout souls and disgraces our sanctuaries.

24. The Altar Bell

a) **When Rung.** The rubrics prescribe that a small bell be rung at the *Sanctus* and at the Elevation. It is also permissible to ring the bell at the *Hanc igitur,* when the priest spreads his hands over the chalice.[33] It is likewise an approved custom to ring the bell at the *Domine non sum dignus* in Mass, but it should not be rung when the priest says these words before the distribution of Communion either during Mass or outside of Mass. When rung during Mass it calls attention to one of the principal parts of the Mass. But when it is rung before the distribution of Communion it is not only unnecessary but also meaningless.[34]

b) **When not Rung.** The bell must not be rung during a Low Mass while a High Mass is being sung in the same church. Nor may it be rung even on Sundays either at the altar of exposition or at any other altar in the church during the time the Blessed Sacrament is

---

31. Fortescue, p. 34.
32. Augustine, *Liturgical Law,* p. 265.
33. S.R.C. 4377.
34. See *Amer. Eccl. Review,* February, 1905, p. 184.

exposed, as during the Forty Hours' Adoration.[35] Moreover, it should not be rung at a side altar while a wedding
or a funeral is taking place. Nor is it rung while the Office
is being recited in choir, nor while the celebrant and
sacred ministers are on the way to the altar for a Solemn
High Mass, or are returning to the sacristy after it, nor,
finally, while a procession is in progress in the church.[36]

c) How Rung. The bell should be rung softly and
gently but sufficiently loud that it can be heard by those
in the rear pews. In ringing the bell abruptness and vio-
lence should be avoided. A single stroke of the bell is
preferable to a prolonged ringing. Thus, at the *Sanctus*
three distinct strokes, not too close together, are given;
and at the *Hanc igitur* one stroke. At the Consecration
the server rings the bell six times in all, once at each of
the four genuflections, and once when the priest elevates the Host, and again when he elevates the Chalice.
The rubric here permits that the bell be rung but twice,
and that continuously from the time the priest begins to
elevate the Host or Chalice till he again replaces it on the
altar. The former is the better method and the one in general use.

d) What It Is. According to the rubrics of the Missal
the altar bell is a small hand bell.[37] Nothing can equal in
appropriateness a simple, single, sweet-toned bell. Bishop
Van der Stappen would tolerate a correctly tuned chime of
three or four small bells, but he hastens to add that the
single bell prescribed by the rubrics is preferable.[38]

e) What It Is Not. Gongs are forbidden.[39] But no less
objectionable are chimes of plates or tubes mounted on a
board, and so-called electric altar chimes which consist of

35. S.R.C. 3151, 10 and 3448, 2.
36. De Carpo-Moretti, 449; *Matters Liturgical,* 126.
37. *Ritus cel.,* VII, 8.
38. Vol. Ill, p. 116. See also *Emmanuel,* June, 1926.
39. ·S.R.C. 4000, 3. The instrument referred to in the decree resembles our gong.

Fig. 8. A permissible   **Fig. 9.** The altar
bell.   bell prescribed by
the rubrics.

tubes operated from a keyboard sunk in the altar step.
Such devices savor of the theater, not of the sanctuary.

25. The Communion Plate or Paten

Owing to the two different practices that obtain, it is
best to treat of the communion plate or paten from the
point of view of the one who holds it.

a) When It Is Held by the Communicants. According to an Instruction issued by the Congregation of the
Sacraments (Mar. 26, 1929), the faithful are to use a
metal plate which they hold under their chin while receiving Holy Communion. They pass the plate from hand to
hand themselves. The server is not directed to have anything to do with it.[40]

b) When It Is Held by the Server. It has long been
a custom in this country and apparently in others, for the
server to hold an unconsecrated paten under the chin of

---

40. This Instruction is given in full in *Matters Liturgical,* 3rd ed. Appendix, pp. 9–12; and
there also will be found valuable comment on it taken from the *Ephemerides Liturgicae,*
1930, pp. 72–74.

the person receiving Holy Communion. He walks at the right of the priest and holds the paten, not in front of, but about two inches below, the chin of each communicant. It must at all times be kept level so that if minute particles fall on it they will not slide off. The paten must never touch the person of a communicant. On returning to the altar the server goes up to the platform with the priest and places the paten on the altar to be purified.

In answer to a question, the Congregation of the Sacraments (Oct., 1930) declared that the use of the paten as described above is in no way prohibited by the decree regarding the use of the communion plate. "Therefore our altar boys, when serving Mass, may continue to hold the paten while Holy Communion is distributed, provided they are careful to keep it horizontal, lest fragments of sacred particles fall off."[41]

The use of either the plate or paten does not do away with the communion cloth which must still be spread at the altar rail. Such things are merely additional precautions to safeguard the fragments of the sacred particles.

26. The Server's Communion: Precedence

As a general rule the server receives Holy Communion before all others. But this statement requires some qualification to bring it into conformity with two important decrees on the subject.[42] These may be briefly summarized as follows:

a) If the server is the usual altar boy, hence a layman, he receives Communion before other laymen, including Sisters; but he does not receive Communion before a cleric in major orders, minor orders, or before one who has received only the tonsure. Nor does he receive Communion before certain privileged persons who are specifically recognized in the liturgy, such as the bridal couple in a nuptial Mass.

---

41. *Amer. Eccl. Review,* Oct., 1931, p. 413.
42. S.R.C. 1074, July 13, 1658; and 4328, June 30, 1915.

b) A server in minor orders receives Communion before other persons in minor orders, but not before those in major orders. The privileged persons referred to above must be given precedence over clerics in minor orders, but not over those in major orders.

c) A layman serving Mass, though not vested in cassock and surplice, receives Holy Communion in the sanctuary, kneeling on the platform of the altar.[43]

When receiving Communion the server holds a cloth, a card, or the communion plate or paten under his chin. He must not use the lower part of the priest's chasuble or stole for a communion cloth.[44]

27. Offering Holy Water

If there is a holy water font or stoup at the sacristy door, it is customary on entering the sanctuary for the server to dip his fingers into it and offer his outstretched fingers to the priest. He makes the sign of the cross and proceeds. If there are several servers, as in High Mass, those who are next to the font take holy water, and each one presents it to his companion. If there is no deacon, the last server presents it to the priest.

If the *Asperges* takes place, holy water is not taken by anyone at the sacristy door. The *Asperges* takes place before the principal Mass on Sunday, and on no other day.

28. Carrying the Missal to the Altar

The rubrics suppose that the Missal to be used in Low Mass is left in the sacristy to be marked by the priest who is to celebrate. Where this is observed the server, walking before the priest, carries the Missal to the altar. He holds the book from below, with one hand at each corner. The opening is toward his left, and the top rests against his breast. At the altar he places it on the bookstand with the

---

43. S.R.C. 4271, 1.
44. Van der Stappen, Vol. V, p. 47.

Fig. 10. Carrying the Missal to the
altar: how it is held.

opening toward the crucifix. The back of a closed Missal is
never turned toward the middle of the altar, whether it be
at the Epistle side or at the Gospel side. The server must
not open the Missal nor turn over its pages.[45] At the end
of Mass he carries it back to the sacristy.

In many churches it is customary not to carry the Missal
to and from the altar. Nor is this practice contrary to the
rubrics. "In regard to the carrying of the Missal from the
sacristy to the altar by the server, the rubric is not categor-
ical (one admitting of no exception) and does not condemn
a contrary practice. . . . The *Baltimore Ceremonial* is right

---

45. S.R.C. 2572 and 3448, 14.

in saying: 'After the priest is vested, the server takes the Missal, unless it is already on the altar.' "[46]

29. Transferring the Missal during Mass

In going for the Missal, and when returning after placing it on the altar, the server walks on the floor. He goes up to the platform, and comes down from it, by the side steps. But while actually carrying the Missal he goes down to the middle by the front steps, and after genuflecting on the floor, he goes up by the front steps and places the book on the altar.[47] At the Epistle side the server stands on the top step till the priest goes to the middle of the altar. After transferring the Missal he likewise stands on the top step at the Gospel side and waits for the priest to begin the Gospel.

Figure 11 shows the path which a server follows in removing the Missal from the Epistle to the Gospel side.

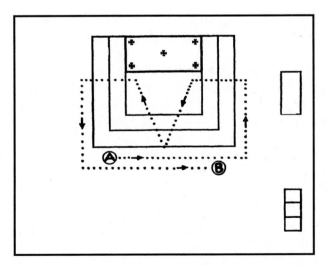

Fig. 11. Transferring the Missal during Mass.

---

46. *Amer. Eccl. Review,* Nov., 1929, p. 513; *Baltimore Cer.,* 9th ed., p. 58.
47. Fortescue, p. 84; Callewaert, p. 158, note 6, and others. The rubrics do not specify how the Missal is carried.

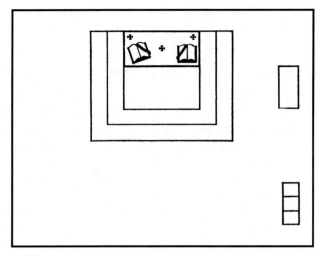

Fig. 12. How the Missal is placed on the altar:
at the Epistle side; at the Gospel side.

At the end of the Epistle he rises from his position at A, and follows the dotted line till he arrives at B, where he stands during the reading of the Gospel.

Figure 12 shows the positions which the Missal should occupy when it is placed at the Epistle and at the Gospel sides, respectively. At the Epistle side the front of the bookstand must be parallel with the front of the altar. At the Gospel side it is never so placed, but it must be turned halfway toward the middle of the altar. The priest is supposed to be partly facing the people while he is reading the Gospel.

30. Turning the Back toward the Altar

A server should be careful not to turn his back directly toward the altar. This is true of every altar, whether the Blessed Sacrament be reserved on it or not. It must not be inferred from this that a server is here directed to walk sideways or backwards in the sanctuary. Far from it.

One of the things this rule implies may be illustrated by a single example, though many might be given. If, after presenting wine and water at the Offertory, the server turns to the right to go back to the credence table, he should there turn to the left when leaving the table to minister at the *Lavabo*. The observance of this rule calls for thoughtfulness on the part of the server, and for deep reverence and respect for God's holy altar.

31. The Elevation Candle

A rubric in the Missal prescribes that in Low Mass a third candle be lit at the *Sanctus,* and that it remain lit till after Communion. It is variously styled the "Sanctus Candle," "Elevation Candle," or "Consecration Candle." Unfortunately this rubric is no longer extensively observed. But where it is observed it is preferable that the candle should not be placed on the altar, nor is it to be held by the server; but it should be placed in a bracket attached to the wall at the Epistle side. Or it may be placed in a candlestick on the credence table, or on the floor, or on the steps of the altar near the server.[48]

"The size of the candlestick and its material obviously depends on the locality. Hartmann mentions as a suitable size a candlestick of 1.50 meter (59 inches), so that it may be visible from the body of the church. Others give the size as that of the Easter candlestick, and suggest that two of the same size be placed respectively on the Epistle and the Gospel side, the latter to be used for the Easter candle."[49]

32. Holding the Chasuble at the Elevation

In any Mass in which there is no deacon the server kneels on the platform and raises slightly the lower

---

48. Martinucci, Vol. I, p. 139; Fortescue, p. 85; De Herdt, Vol. I, p. 405; Callewaert, p. 162; Van der Stappen, Vol. III, p. 64; De Carpo-Moretti, p. 201. The nonuse of this beautiful symbolical candle is permitted where the custom obtains. S.R.C. 4029, 2.
49. *Amer. Eccl. Review,* Vol. 51, 1914, p. 488. For an illustration of two such candlesticks see the *Liturgical Arts Review,* Vol. I, No. 2, 1932, p. 60.

part of the chasuble during the actual elevation of the Host and Chalice, but not during the four genuflections. During the genuflections he does not touch the chasuble. At each elevation it is held but momentarily, its lower part being raised about four or five inches. The chasuble must not be drawn outward, away from the priest; nor should it be pulled or tugged even slightly. While kneeling on the platform, the server does not strike his breast, nor does he make the sign of the cross. If the platform is narrow, he may kneel on the top step.

a) If there is but one server, he kneels on the edge of the platform at the right of the priest. After the first genuflection at the consecration of the Host or Chalice, he takes hold of the chasuble at the middle of the lower rim with his left hand, and with his right he rings the bell. He releases the chasuble the moment the Host or Chalice is replaced on the altar.

b) If there are two servers, one kneels at each side of the priest, and they both hold the lower rim of the chasuble, one with his right hand, the other with his left. In holding the chasuble it is important that the hands be held equally high. To secure uniformity the server at the left should be guided by the one at the right. With practice even the smallest altar boy can be taught to perform this ceremony in a becoming manner.

c) At each of the four genuflections the servers bow (bow M). At each elevation they look upon the Sacred Species and say: "My Lord and my God"—a prayer richly indulgenced by Pope Pius X.

d) At the Elevation some authorities do not direct the server to genuflect either before he goes up to kneel on the platform or again on his return to the floor. Others prescribe both.[50] Others, again, direct that a genuflection be made only on the server's return to the floor.[51] This practice is more consistent with the general rule that

---

50. Van der Stappen, Vol. V, p. 46.
51. Callewaert, p. 163.

while the Blessed Sacrament is on the corporal the server genuflects before going up to the platform for any purpose and again on returning to the floor.

33. Special Ceremonies for Special Seasons and Occasions

a) On certain days especially in Lent and on the Ember Days there may be several Epistles or Lessons. After each Lesson the server answers *Deo gratias,* except after the fifth Lesson on those Saturdays that are Ember Days. The server will know that these Lessons are to be read whenever the priest, after the *Kyrie eleison,* does not turn around and say *Dominus vobiscum* but goes directly to the Missal. The regular Epistle of the Mass comes as usual after the *Dominus vobiscum* which is always said at the middle of the altar. When, on these days, the priest says *Flectamus genua* while at the Epistle side, the server answers *Levate.*

b) Psalm 42, a part of the prayers said at the foot of the altar, is omitted in Masses said in black vestments, and in those said in violet vestments from Passion Sunday till Holy Thursday.

c) On certain penitential days in Advent, Lent, on the Ember Days, and on some other occasions, the deacon and subdeacon wear folded chasubles. With the assistance of the second acolyte the subdeacon takes off his chasuble during the last Collect, and he puts it on again when he has received the celebrant's blessing after the Epistle. It is taken off and put on at the bench.

The deacon, assisted by the first acolyte, goes to the credence table and takes off the folded chasuble as soon as the celebrant begins to read the Gospel. He puts on a broad stole over his real stole and remains so vested till after Communion. After he has carried the Missal to the Epistle side, he again goes to the credence table and takes off the broad stole and puts on the chasuble.[52]

---

52. See *Rub. gen.,* XIX, 6, and Fortescue, p. 271.

d) The Passion is read or sung in four Masses during Holy Week; viz., on Palm Sunday, on the Tuesday and Wednesday following, and on Good Friday. *Dominus vobiscum,* etc., are omitted at the beginning, but *Laus tibi Christe* is said at the end. This is said when the priest has gone to the Gospel side a second time and has finished reading the narrative of the Passion. When finished, he kisses the book, except on Good Friday.

e) At the end of Mass during Easter week the priest says *Ite missa est, alleluia, alleluia.* The server answers *Deo gratias, alleluia, alleluia.*

f) On All Souls' Day and on Christmas Day a priest may say three Masses, and on Sundays and Holy Days of Obligation two. On such occasions, when the Masses are said on the same altar, the priest does not purify the chalice till the last Mass. The server, therefore, should transfer the Missal as usual, but he should present wine and water for the ablutions only in the last Mass.

g) From Easter Sunday till Ascension Day the Paschal candle is lit at Solemn Mass and Vespers (at High Mass and sung Vespers) on all Sundays, and if customary, on other days and solemnities that are celebrated during the Easter season.[53] It may also be lit at a parochial or community Low Mass that takes the place of a High Mass. But it must never be lit at a Mass celebrated in violet or in black vestments.[54]

It is not lit during Benediction of the Blessed Sacrament.[55] But if Vespers immediately precedes Benediction, and the candle was lit during Vespers, it remains lighted during Benediction.[56]

On Ascension Day it is extinguished after the first Gospel, and it is no longer used.

h) In Requiem Masses the clergy may, and generally do, hold lighted candles as indicated on pages 67 and 102

---

53. S.R.C. 235, 11.
54. Merati, 1, 4, 10.
55. S.R.C. 3479, 3.
56. S.R.C. 4383, 1.

of this book.[57] The rubric, however, does not absolutely prescribe the distribution of candles, but merely says "if candles are to be distributed."[58]

34. Postures during the Credo

Should the servers kneel or stand while the celebrant is reciting the *Credo* in Low Mass and in High Mass (*Missa Cantata*)? This question has been asked repeatedly. Its answer is contained in a General Rubric in the Missal *(Rubr. gen.* XVII, 2). The best authorities[59] are practically unanimous in prescribing that the servers kneel during the *Credo,* as they are directed to do on pp. 44, 55, and 64 of this book.

As already stated, O'Connell prescribes a kneeling posture in both Low Mass and High Mass, but in the latter he adds the following footnote: "Some authors, by analogy with (Solemn) High Mass, direct them to stand when not engaged in any special duty. If they do, they must (a) genuflect when the priest recites *Et incarnatus* of the Creed, (b) kneel from after the Sanctus until after the Elevation, (c) kneel, for the Blessing" (Vol. III, p. 201).

---

57. *Ritus Cel. Missam, XIII,* 3.
58. *Ritus ser., XIII,* 3; Augustine *Liturgical Law,* p. 287.
59. Among them Wapelhorst (10 ed.) sections 131, n. 6, and 155, n. 5; Fortescue (6th ed.), pp. 84 and 144; De Carpo-Moretti (1932), sections 445 and 868; O'Connell, *The Celebration of Mass* (1940), Vol. II, p. 194; and Vol. III, p. 202; Callewaert, *Caeremoniale* (1934), pp. 161 and 229. It would be easy to add to this list.

Chapter 2

Prayers at Mass

THE SERVER KNEELS erect with hands joined unless otherwise directed. At each cross ✠ he makes the sign of the cross with the priest.

Priest: In nómine ✠ Patris, et Fílii, et Spíritus Sancti. Amen.

Antiphon

Priest: Introíbo ad altáre Dei.
Server: Ad Deum, qui laetíficat juventútem meam.

Psalm 42

Priest: Júdica me, Deus, et discérne causam meam de gente non sancta: ab hómine iníquo et dolóso érue me.
Server: Quia tu es, Deus, fortitúdo mea: quare me repulísti, et quare tristis incédo, dum afflígit me inimícus?
Priest: Emítte lucem tuam et veritátem tuam: ipsa me deduxérunt, et adduxérunt in montem sanctum tuum et in tabernácula tua.
Server: Et introíbo ad altáre Dei: ad Deum, qui laetíficat juventútem meam.

Priest: Confitébor tibi in cíthara, Deus, Deus meus: quare tristis es, ánima mea, et quare contúrbas me?

Server: Spera in Deo, quóniam adhuc confitébor illi: salutáre vultus mei, et Deus meus.

The server bows his head with the priest while the latter says:

Priest: Glória Patri, et Fílio, et Spirítui Sancto.

Server: Sicut erat in princípio, et nunc, et semper: et in saécula saéculorum. Amen.

Priest: Introíbo ad altáre Dei.

Server: Ad Deum qui laetíficat juventútem meam.

The above psalm is omitted in Masses said in black vestments, and in Masses said in violet vestments from Passion Sunday till Holy Thursday. In such Masses only the Antiphon is said.

Priest: Adjutórium nostrum ✝ in nómine Dómini.

Server: Qui fecit caelum et terram.

The Confiteor

The priest says the *Confiteor* during which the server kneels erect, neither bowing his head nor striking his breast. At the end of the *Confiteor* he bows his head, and turning slightly toward the priest he says:

Server: Misereátur tui omnípotens Deus, et, dimíssis peccátis tuis, perdúcat te ad vitam aetérnam.

Priest: Amen.

The server now bows (bow M) and says the *Confiteor* distinctly and without haste. At the words *tibi pater* and *te pater* he turns partly toward the priest. At *mea culpa, mea culpa, mea maxima culpa,* he strikes his breast three times. He remains bowed till the *Amen* following the *Misereatur vestri.*

Server: Confíteor Deo omnipoténti, beátae Maríae semper Vírgini, beáto Michaéli Archángelo, beáto Joánni Baptístae, sanctis Apóstolis Petro et Paulo, ómnibus Sanctis, et tibi, pater: quia peccávi nimis cogitatióne, verbo et ópere: mea culpa, mea culpa, mea máxima culpa. Ideo precor beátam Maríam semper Vírginem, beátum Michaélem Archángelum, beátum Joánnem Baptístam, sanctos Apóstolos Petrum et Paulum, omnes Sanctos, et te, pater, oráre pro me ad Dóminum, Deum nostrum.

Priest: Misereátur vestri omnípotens Deus, et, dimíssis peccátis vestris, perdúcat vos ad vitam aetérnam.

Server: Amen. (The server now kneels erect.)

Priest: Indulgéntiam, ✠ absolutiónem et remissiónem peccatórum nostrórum tríbuat nobis omnípotens et miséricors Dóminus.

Server: Amen.

The server bows moderately and remains bowed.

Priest: Deus, tu convérsus vivificábis nos.
Server: Et plebs tua laetábitur in te.
Priest: Osténde nobis, Dómine, misericórdiam tuam.
Server: Et salutáre tuum da nobis.
Priest: Dómine, exáudi oratiónem meam.
Server: Et clamor meus ad te véniat.
Priest: Dóminus vobíscum.
Server: Et cum spíritu tuo. (Server now kneels erect.)

The priest goes up to the altar, and goes to the Epistle side to read the Introit. He begins this by making the sign of the cross ✠, except when he wears black vestments. The Kyrie follows the Introit.

Priest: Kyrie eléison.
Server: Kyrie eléison.
Priest: Kyrie eléison.
Server: Christe eléison.
Priest: Christe eléison.
Server: Christe eléison.
Priest: Kyrie eléison.
Server: Kyrie eléison.
Priest: Kyrie eléison.

The Gloria

(The *Gloria* is omitted when the priest wears black or violet vestments.)

Glória in excélsis *Deo.* Et in terra pax homínibus bonae voluntátis. Laudámus te. Benedícimus te. *Adorámus te.* Glorificámus te. *Grátias ágimus tibi* propter magnam glóriam tuam. Dómine Deus, Rex caeléstis, Deus Pater omnípotens. Dómine Fili unigénite, *Jesu Christe.* Dómine Deus, Agnus Dei, Fílius Patris. Qui tollis peccáta mundi, miserére nobis. Qui tollis peccáta mundi, *súscipe deprecatiónem nostram.* Qui sedes ad déxteram Patris, miserére nobis. Quóniam tu solus sanctus. Tu solus Dóminus. Tu solus Altíssimus, *Jesu Christe.* Cum Sancto Spíritu, in glória Dei Patris. Amen.

Priest: Dóminus vobíscum.
Server: Et cum spíritu tuo.
Priest: Per ómnia saécula saeculórum.
Server: Amen.

At the end of the Epistle:

Server: Deo grátias. (Server goes for the Missal.)

At the beginning of the Gospel:

Priest: Dóminus vobíscum.
Server: Et cum spíritu tuo.

Priest: Sequéntia sancti Evangélii, etc. ✝ ✝ ✝.
Server: Glória tibi, Dómine.

At the end of the Gospel:

Server: Laus tibi, Christe.

The Credo

Credo in unum Deum, Patrem omnipoténtem, factórem caeli et terrae, visibílium ómnium et invisibílium. Et in unum Dóminum *Jesum Christum,* Fílium Dei unigénitum. Et ex Patre natum ante ómnia saécula. Deum de Deo, lumen de lúmine, Deum verum de Deo vero. Génitum non factum, consubstantiálem Patri: per quem ómnia facta sunt. Qui propter nos hómines et propter nostram salútem descéndit de caelis. *Et incarnátus est de Spíritu Sancto ex María Vírgine: Et homo factus est.* Crucifíxus étiam pro nobis: sub Póntio Piláto passus, et sepúltus est. Et resurréxit tértia die, secúndum Scriptúras. Et ascéndit in caelum: sedet ad déxteram Patris. Et íterum ventúrus est cum glória judicáre vivos et mórtuos: cujus regni non erit finis. Et in Spíritum Sanctum, Dóminum et vivificántem: qui ex Patre Filióque procédit. Qui cum Patre et Fílio *simul adorátur* et conglorificátur: qui locútus est per Prophétas. Et unam sanctam cathólicam et apostólicam Ecclésiam. Confíteor unum baptísma in remissiónem peccatórum. Et exspécto resurrectiónem mortuórum. Et vitam ventúri saéculi. Amen.

After the Gospel or Credo

Priest: Dóminus vobíscum.
Server: Et cum spíritu tuo.

After the Lavabo

Priest: Oráte, fratres: ut meum ac vestrum sacrifícium acceptábile fiat apud Deum Patrem omnipoténtem.

Then, when the priest again faces the altar:

Server: Suscípiat Dóminus sacrifícium de mánibus tuis ad laudem et glóriam nóminis sui, ad utilitátem quoque nostram, totiúsque Ecclésiae suae sanctae.

The Preface

There are fifteen Prefaces. The following one is said on Trinity Sunday and on all Sundays throughout the year that have no proper Preface:

Priest: Per ómnia saécula saeculórum.
Server: Amen.
Priest: Dóminus vobíscum.
Server: Et cum spíritu tuo.
Priest: Sursum corda.
Server: Habémus ad Dóminum.
Priest: Grátias agámus Dómino Deo nostro.
Server: Dignum et justum est.
Priest: Vere dignum et justum est, aequum et salutáre, nos tibi semper et ubíque grátias ágere: Dómine sancte, Pater omnípotens, aetérne Deus: Qui cum unigénito Fílio tuo et Spíritu Sancto unus es Deus, unus es Dóminus: non in uníus singularitáte persónae, sed in uníus Trinitáte substántiae. Quod enim de tua glória, revelánte te, crédimus, hoc de Fílio tuo, hoc de Spíritu Sancto sine differéntia discretiónis sentímus. Ut in confessióne verae sempiternaéque Deitátis, et in persónis propríetas, et in esséntia únitas, et in majestáte adorétur aequálitas. Quam laudant Angeli atque Archángeli, Chérubim quoque ac Séraphim: qui non cessant clamáre quotídie, una voce dicéntes:

Sanctus, sanctus, sanctus, Dóminus Deus Sábaoth. Pleni sunt caeli et terra glória tua. Hosánna in excélsis. Benedíctus qui venit in nómine Dómini. Hosánna in excélsis.

Shortly before the Consecration, when the priest spreads his hands over the chalice, the server rings the bell and kneels on the platform beside the priest.

Before the Pater Noster

Priest: Per ómnia saécula saeculórum.
Server: Amen.
Priest: Orémus: Praecéptis salutáribus móniti, et divína institutióne formáti, audémus dícere:

Pater noster, qui es in caelis: Sanctificétur nomen tuum: Advéniat regnum tuum: Fiat volúntas tua, sicut in caelo, et in terra. Panem nostrum quotidiánum da nobis hódie: Et dimítte nobis débita nostra, sicut et nos dimíttimus debitóribus nostris. Et ne nos indúcas in tentatiónem.

Server: Sed líbera nos a malo.

After a Brief Pause

Priest: Per ómnia saécula saeculórum.
Server: Amen.
Priest: Pax Dómini sit semper vobíscum.
Server: Et cum spíritu tuo.

At the Agnus Dei

The server bows his head and strikes his breast at the same time that the priest does.

At the Domine Non Sum Dignus

The server rings the bell three times. He does not strike his breast.

After Communion

Priest: Dóminus vobíscum.
Server: Et cum spíritu tuo.
Priest: Per ómnia saécula saeculórum.
Server: Amen.
Priest: Dóminus vobíscum.
Server: Et cum spíritu tuo.
Priest: Ite missa est (If the *Gloria* was said in the Mass).
Priest: Benedicámus Dómino (If *Gloria* was not said).
Server: Deo grátias. (See Section 31d.)
Priest: Benedícat vos omnípotens Deus, Pater, ✠ et Fílius, et Spíritus Sanctus.
Server: Amen.

In Masses for the Dead

Priest: Requiéscant in pace.
Server: Amen.

At the Beginning of the Last Gospel

Priest: Dóminus vobíscum.
Server: Et cum spíritu tuo.
Priest: Inítium ✠ ✠ ✠ sancti Evangélii secúndum Joánnem.
Server: Glória tibi, Dómine.

At the End of the Last Gospel

Server: Deo grátias.

During the Prayers after Mass the server kneels on the lowest step, at the right of the priest.

Chapter 3

Low Mass

LOW MASS WITH ONE SERVER

IT IS IMPORTANT THAT every altar boy should be able to serve Mass alone. No one should consider himself a server until he can do this, and do it well. More than twenty of the thirty-four Sections included under "Common Ceremonial Actions" apply in Low Mass. It is presumed that the server is familiar with these. The following general rules will also be helpful:

1. The server's usual place is at the side opposite the book, except when the last Gospel is read from the card.

2. He kneels during the whole Mass, except during the two Gospels, or when performing some duty. He kneels on the lowest step,[1] except during the opening prayers and at the Elevation.

Particular Instructions

The server should be in the sacristy at least ten minutes before Mass begins. He should make a short meditation before the Blessed Sacrament, and put on his cassock and surplice. He sees to it that the cruets, dish, and finger towel are on the credence table, that the altar cover or dust cloth is removed, that the three altar cards are in their proper places, that the two candles are lit,

---

1. If there is but one step, some authorities direct the server to kneel on the floor during the whole Mass. This is not prescribed by any rubric.

and finally, if such be the custom, that the Missal is on the stand at the Epistle side.

On the Way to the Altar.   When the priest is vested, the server takes the Missal, if it is not already on the altar, bows with him to the crucifix (bow H), and precedes him to the altar. At the sacristy door, where it is customary, he takes holy water and offers it to the priest. Both make the sign of the cross. If there is a bell at the sacristy door, he rings it gently in passing.

If, on the way to the altar where Mass is to be said, the server passes before the altar on which the Blessed Sacrament is reserved, he genuflects with the priest. In passing before an altar on which the Blessed Sacrament is exposed, or where the distribution of Holy Communion is taking place, both kneel, bow moderately, and proceed. In passing an altar at the Elevation, both kneel till the Elevation is finished.

At the Altar.   On arriving near the middle of the altar, if the entrance is from the Epistle side, the server steps back to permit the priest to pass between him and the altar steps. He stands at the right of the priest and receives his biretta. He genuflects when the priest either bows or genuflects. He puts the biretta on the credence table or in some other convenient place, and places the Missal on the stand. In doing this he goes up to the platform, and returns again to the floor, by the side steps. He then goes toward the Gospel side, taking care to genuflect when he passes the middle of the altar. He remains standing, about two feet from the middle and one foot from the lowest step.

Mass Begins.   When the priest comes down to the floor to begin Mass, the server kneels erect and makes the sign of the cross with him. He answers the prayers with great distinctness, avoiding all haste. He bows (bow H) at the *Gloria Patri,* and makes the sign of the cross at *Adjutorium nostrum in nomine Domini.* During the

priest's *Confiteor* he does not bow, nor does he strike his
breast. While saying *Misereatur tui,* etc., he turns slightly
toward the priest and bows (bow H). Then bowing (bow M)
toward the altar he says the *Confiteor,* At the words *tibi
pater* and *te pater* he turns slightly toward the priest. He
strikes his breast three times at the words *mea culpa, mea
culpa, mea maxima culpa.* He remains bowed till he has
answered *Amen* after the *Misereatur vestri.* Then kneeling
erect he makes the sign of the cross at *Indulgentiam,* etc.
During the remainder of the introductory prayers he bows
moderately (bow M) toward the altar. When the priest goes
up to the altar, the server rises. He does not genuflect but
goes directly to his place toward the end of the lowest step
and kneels.

At the Kyrie. At the *Kyrie* he answers *Kyrie eleison*
once, then *Christe eleison* twice, and again *Kyrie eleison*
once. After *Dominus vobiscum,* whenever it is said, he
answers *Et cum spiritu tuo.* After *Per omnia saecula
saeculorum* he always answers *Amen.* During the Epistle
the priest rests his hands upon the Missal or upon the
altar. When he finishes reading it he raises his left hand
slightly or lowers his voice. This is a sign for the server to
answer *Deo gratias.* He immediately rises, genuflects at
the middle, and transfers the Missal to the Gospel side as
directed in Section 29 of "Common Ceremonial Actions."
On certain days more than one Epistle or Lesson may be
read. See Section 33a. After placing the Missal on the
Gospel side, the server stands on the top step. He answers
the prayers at the beginning of the Gospel, and makes the
triple sign of the cross with the priest. At the opening
words of the Gospel, if the Holy Name of Jesus occurs, he
bows (bow H); if it does not occur, he does not bow. Turning to his right he goes down to the floor and goes to the
Epistle side. During the Gospel he stands partly facing the
priest. At the end of the Gospel he answers *Laus tibi,
Christe,* and kneels. He does not stand during the *Credo.* If
the *Credo* is said, the server bows (bow H) when the priest
genuflects at the words *Et incarnatus est.*

At the Offertory. When the priest removes the veil from the chalice the server rises and, without genuflecting, goes directly to the credence table for the cruets.[2] He takes the wine cruet in his right hand, and the water cruet in his left. See Section 18. He goes up to the top step, and when the priest approaches he bows to him (bow H). He presents the wine cruet, and immediately transfers the water cruet to his right hand and receives back the wine cruet with his left. He kisses each cruet both before presenting it and again on receiving it back. On receiving the water cruet he bows (bow H) and returns to the credence table. In presenting the cruets and at the *Lavabo* bow H is made four times in all.

At the Lavabo. The server places the finger towel unfolded on his left arm. He takes the water cruet in his right hand and the basin or dish in his left and goes up again to the top step. He bows when the priest approaches and gently pours a little water over his fingers. The cruet is held about an inch above the tips of the priest's index fingers. In pouring the water the cruet should not be moved about in circles. He turns to his right to enable the priest to reach the towel the more easily. On receiving back the towel he bows and replaces the cruet, dish, and towel on the credence table. The cruets are placed on the table, not on the wet dish. He then goes directly to his place at the Epistle side, and kneels. At the *Orate fratres* he waits till the priest has turned again toward the altar, then, without bowing, he answers *Suscipiat Dominus,* etc.

At the Preface. He answers the versicles at the beginning of the Preface, and rings the bell three times at the *Sanctus.* See Section 24c. Without genuflecting, he now goes to the Epistle side to light the elevation candle, if one is to be lit. See Section 31.

---

2. The method of presenting the cruets which is here given, as well as the ceremonies at the *Lavabo,* is that found in our *Baltimore Ceremonial,* and in De Herdt, Callewaert, Van der Stappen, and others.

At the Elevation. At the prayer *Hanc igitur* the priest spreads his hands over the chalice. The server rings the bell, rises, and goes toward the middle to a point just below where he is to kneel on the platform. Then, without genuflecting, he goes up and kneels on the edge of the platform at the right of the priest. See Sections 24 and 32. He rings the bell once at each of the four genuflections, and once at each elevation. With his left hand he raises slightly the lower edge of the chasuble during the actual elevation of the Host and of the Chalice, but not during the four genuflections. At each of the genuflections he bows (bow M). After the last one he rises, turns toward the left, descends to the floor, genuflects, and goes to his place. See Section 30.

After the Elevation. He remains kneeling till Communion. In the meantime he answers at the *Pater Noster,* and bows (bow H) and strikes his breast with the priest at the *Agnus Dei.* At the *Domine non sum dignus* he rings the bell once each time the words are said, but he does not strike his breast.

If Communion Is Not Distributed. When the priest removes the pall from the chalice, the server rises and goes directly to the credence table for the cruets. He takes the wine cruet in his right hand and the water cruet in his left. He goes to the side steps, genuflects, and ascends to the top step. He bows (bow M) while the priest receives the Precious Blood. Then, going up close to the priest, he pours wine into the chalice when the priest holds it toward him. He holds the cruet about an inch above the chalice and pours wine gently into it till the priest raises it slightly as a sign to stop. Then, turning to his right he goes back to his place on the top step. When the priest approaches for the second ablution the server bows (bow H) to him and pours first wine and then water over his fingers, not touching them with the cruets. The bow is repeated. The cruets are not kissed at either ablution. At the second ablution the cruets are held close to the priest's fingers. The wine and water should be poured slowly, and in doing so the cruet must not be moved around in circles. After placing the cruets on the credence table the server extinguishes the elevation candle, if one were lit after the *Sanctus.*

If Communion Is Distributed. The server, instead of going to the credence table for the cruets, kneels on the lowest step at the Epistle side, facing the Gospel side. When the priest has consumed the Precious Blood, the server bows (bow M) and says the *Confiteor.* Here read carefully Section 24a and all of Sections 25 and 26. If the server with a paten accompanies the priest during the distribution of Holy Communion, he walks at the priest's right. On returning to the altar he goes up with the priest and places the paten on the altar near the corporal and waits for it to be purified if the priest does it at once. Then receiving the paten he genuflects and kneels on the lowest side step at the Epistle side till the priest closes the tabernacle door. But if the paten is not purified at once, the server genuflects and goes down and kneels as directed above. The paten would then be removed from the altar after the ablutions.

After the Ablutions. The server does not carry the veil of the chalice to the Gospel side. He brings back the Missal to the Epistle side, and in doing so he observes the same general directions as when he carried it to the Gospel side. See Section 29. After the removal of the book he kneels at his usual place at the Gospel side and answers the prayers up to, and including, the beginning of the Last Gospel.

If the Last Gospel is to be read from the Missal, the priest will leave the book open. Immediately after answering at the *Ite missa est* the server transfers the Missal as at the first Gospel. If the blessing is being given as he passes the middle, he kneels there to receive it. Otherwise he places the book on the altar and receives the blessing while kneeling on the lowest side step near the Missal at the Gospel side. Then rising he makes the responses and does everything as at the first Gospel. He then goes to the Epistle side where he stands turned somewhat toward the priest. At the end of the Last Gospel he says *Deo gratias.*

During the Prayers after Mass.   The server kneels, not on the floor, but on the lowest step beside the priest.[3] During these prayers, if the Missal had been carried to the Gospel side and another Mass is to follow, the server now carries the book and stand back to the Epistle side. If he is to take the Missal back to the sacristy with him, he removes it from the stand and kneels beside the priest. If the Missal is at the Epistle side, it will be time enough to get it when the priest begins the prayer to St. Michael. But if the server is not to take the Missal to the sacristy, he remains kneeling beside the priest till the end of the prayers.

When the priest goes up to the altar to get the chalice the server goes for the biretta. When the priest descends to the floor the server hands him the biretta. The server genuflects whether the priest bows or genuflects, and precedes him to the sacristy. He bows (bow H) with the priest to the crucifix, and helps him to unvest, if he so wishes. In extinguishing the candles and caring for the cruets he observes what is said in Sections 10 and 19.

LOW MASS FOR THE DEAD

1. The Psalm *Judica* is omitted.
2. Neither the cruets nor any other article is kissed.
3. The breast is not struck at the *Agnus Dei.*
4. Instead of *Ite missa est* the priest says *Requiescant in pace,* and the server answers *Amen.*

---

3. Wapelhorst, p. 157; Menghini, p. 23; De Carpo-Moretti, p. 203; Callewaert, p. 167.

LOW MASS IN THE PRESENCE OF THE BLESSED SACRAMENT EXPOSED

1. The bell is not rung at any part of the Mass.

2. Neither the cruets nor any other article is kissed.

3. At the *Lavabo* both priest and server stand on the floor while the priest washes his hands. The priest faces the people; the server faces the priest.

4. On arriving at the altar, and on leaving it after Mass, both priest and server kneel on both knees and bow (bow M). All genuflections made during Mass are made on one knee only.[4]

5. A genuflection is made on the floor before going up to the altar for any purpose and again after descending. When transferring the Missal, however, the server genuflects only when passing the middle of the altar.[5]

NUPTIAL LOW MASS

Owing to local customs the ceremonies that accompany weddings differ somewhat in matters of minor importance.

The following things should be prepared: (a) a small plate for the ring; (b) the maniple; (c) the holy-water vessel and sprinkler. The first two may be placed on the altar, the last on the platform or elsewhere.

1. The marriage ceremony proper takes place as soon as the priest goes to the altar. The bride and groom kneel on the edge of the platform. The priest, with the server at his right, faces them. Shortly after the bride and groom have joined their right hands the priest sprinkles them with holy water. The server will have the sprinkler ready.

2. The ring is then blessed. During this ceremony the priest may either face the altar or the bridal couple. In the latter case the server holds the dish with the ring on it. In either case he faces in the same direction that the priest does.

---

4. S.R.C. 3426, 6.
5. S.R.C. 3975, I, 1–2.

Priest:	Adjutórium nostrum in nómine Dómini.
Server:	Qui fecit caelum et terram.
Priest:	Dómine, exáudi oratiónem meam.
Server:	Et clamor meus ad te véniat.
Priest:	Dóminus vobíscum.
Server:	Et cum spíritu tuo.
Priest:	Orémus, etc. . . . Per Christum Dóminum nostrum.
Server:	Amen.

The ring is then sprinkled with holy water, and the bridegroom puts it on the bride's finger.

Priest:	Confírma hoc, Deus, quod operátus es in nobis.
Server:	A templo sancto tuo quod est in Jerúsalem.
Priest:	Kyrie eléison.
Server:	Christe eléison.
Priest:	Kyrie eléison.
Priest:	Pater noster . . . et ne nos indúcas in tentatiónem.
Server:	Sed líbera nos a malo.
Priest:	Salvos fac servos tuos.
Server:	Deus meus, sperántes in te.
Priest:	Mitte eis, Dómine, auxílium de sancto.
Server:	Et de Sion tuére eos.
Priest:	Esto eis, Dómine, turris fortitudinis.
Server:	A fácie inimíci.
Priest:	Dómine, exáudi oratiónem meam.
Server:	Et clamor meus ad te véniat.
Priest:	Dóminus vobíscum.
Server:	Et cum spíritu tuo.
Priest:	Orémus, etc. . . . Per Christum Dóminum nostrum.
Server:	Amen.

The priest puts on the maniple; the server puts away the holy water and the plate. Mass begins.

3. At the *Sed libera nos a malo* after the *Pater Noster,* the priest goes toward the Epistle side and stands facing the bridal couple. The server genuflects, goes up to the

platform, and takes the Missal from the stand. He holds it standing in front of he priest. Two prayers are read; at the end of each the server answers *Amen*. At the end of the second he replaces the Missal on the stand and goes to his place.

4. As soon as he has answered *Deo gratias* after the *Benedicamus Domino* or *Ite missa est* he again takes the Missal from the stand and holds it open before the priest. One short prayer is read, at the end of which the server answers *Amen*. The priest may then address the newly married couple. He sprinkles them with holy water, and Mass is concluded as usual.

In some places the server, on the two occasions when he is directed to hold the book before the priest, does not take the Missal that is on the altar but a different one, or a Sacristy Ritual, or a large type stately volume like Father O'Connell's *Benedictionale*.[6]

LOW MASS OF A BISHOP

There should be two servers at a bishop's Mass. There will probably also be one or two priests or clerics who act as chaplains. In addition to the ordinary ceremonies of Low Mass the servers observe the following:

1. Four candles are lit on the altar, unless otherwise directed.

2. Before Mass two candles in candlesticks are placed on the credence table. These are lit at the *Sanctus* and extinguished after Communion. During this time the servers with their candles kneel in their usual places in front of the altar. Instead of the servers, however, two

---

6. In the treatise here given on the Nuptial Mass the writer has in mind the usual wedding ceremony as described in Wapelhorst's *Compendium,* 401, and *Matters Liturgical,* 794. The rubrics are silent as to where the priest and server stand, whether at the altar or at the prie-dieu. Nor is anything prescribed as to where the bride and groom kneel either during the ceremony or during the Mass. For the preferences of other authors see O'Kane's *The Rubrics of the Roman Ritual,* 1030, and Fortescue's *The Roman Rite,* p. 433. Canon 1100 [1917 Code] permits the retention of *praiseworthy customs* in connection with the marriage rite. In such matters Wapelhorst and *Matters Liturgical* are safe guides.

regular torch-bearers may be employed for this purpose. They would have no other duties.

3. The bishop may vest at the altar. He puts on in order the amice, alb, cincture, pectoral cross, stole, and chasuble. Except in Requiem Masses he does not put on the maniple before Mass, but puts it on when he says *Indulgentiam* at the foot of the altar.

4. The servers present water three times for the bishop to wash his hands: (a) Before vesting, (b) At *Lavabo.* (c) After second ablution.

If the celebrant is the bishop of the diocese, or an archbishop within his own province, or a Cardinal anywhere outside of Rome, the servers kneel while he washes his hands; if not, they remain standing.

5. After the *Gloria* the bishop says *Pax vobis* instead of *Dominus vobiscum*. The answer is the same, *Et cum spiritu tuo.*

6. If there are no chaplains, the cruets are handed to the bishop and kissed as usual; if handed to a chaplain they are not kissed.

7. If there are chaplains the servers do not kneel on the platform at the Elevation.

8. The following versicles precede the blessing at the end of Mass:

Bishop: Sit nomen Dómini benedíctum.
Servers: Ex hoc nunc et usque in saéculum.
Bishop: Adjutórium nostrum in nómine Dómini.
Servers: Qui fecit caelum et terram.
Bishop: Benedícat vos omnípotens Deus Pa ✛ ter, et
            Fí ✛ lius, et Spíritus ✛ Sanctus.
Servers: Amen.

LOW MASS WITH TWO SERVERS

In parochial Masses and on solemn occasions two servers are permitted in Low Mass.[7] More than two should not be employed.

---

7. S.R.C. 3059, 7.

1. The servers kneel during the entire Mass, except during the two Gospels or when performing some duty, as will be explained in the proper place.

2. When one server goes to carry anything from one place to another, the other server stands.[8]

3. Their place during Mass is at the opposite ends of the lowest front step facing the altar. But on the first three occasions mentioned below they remain near the middle, leaving room for the priest between them:

a) Before the priest comes down to the floor to begin Mass.

b) During the introductory prayers.

c) During the prayers after Mass.

d) During the distribution of Communion they kneel on the side steps facing each other, unless one of them with a paten accompanies the celebrant at the communion rail. If two priests distribute Communion, each server accompanies a priest. See Section 25.

4. The position of the first server is at the Epistle side, that of the second at the Gospel side. They never change places. Whether they are in front of the altar or at the side, the first server is always at the right of the second.

It is presumed that each server is familiar with the ceremonies of "Low Mass with One Server." The two servers in this Mass merely divide up the duties that are there assigned to one.

Particular Instructions

The servers should be in the sacristy at least ten minutes before Mass begins. After making a short adoration before the Blessed Sacrament they vest in cassock and surplice. The first server assists the priest to vest, and the second sees that the cruets, dish, and finger towel are on the credence table, that the altar cover is removed, that the three altar cards are in their proper places, that two candles are lit, and finally, if such be the custom, that the Missal is on the stand at the Epistle side.

---

8. Fortescue, Menghini.

On the Way to the Altar.   When the priest is vested, the first server takes the Missal, if it is not already on the altar. Both bow with the priest to the crucifix (bow H) and walk before him to the altar. If there is a holy water stoup at the door, the server for whom it is the more convenient takes holy water and presents it to the priest and to the other server. All make the sign of the cross and proceed. If there is a bell at the door, one of the servers rings it gently in passing.

At the Altar.   The servers enter the sanctuary side by side, the first at the right of the second. If the entrance is from the Gospel side, the second server, on arriving at the middle, steps back to permit the priest to pass between him and the lowest step. But if the entrance is from the Epistle side, the above remark applies to the first server. They genuflect beside the priest when the latter either bows or genuflects. If the server carries the Missal he does everything as directed in "Low Mass with One Server." But if the Missal is already on the altar he puts the biretta on the credence table or on the bench and returns to his place. Both servers remain standing where they genuflected, till the priest comes down from the platform to begin Mass.

Mass Begins.   When the priest descends to the floor the servers kneel erect, about one foot from the lowest step. After making the sign of the cross with the priest they answer the prayers with great distinctness, avoiding all haste. They bow (bow H) at the *Gloria Patri* and make the sign of the cross at *Adjutorium nostrum in nomine Domini.* They do not bow, nor do they strike their breasts, during the priest's *Confiteor.* While saying *Misereatur tui,* etc., they turn slightly toward the priest and bow (bow H). Then bowing (bow M) toward the altar, they say the *Confiteor.* At the words *tibi pater* and *te pater* they bow slightly toward the priest. They strike their breasts three times at the words *mea culpa, mea culpa, mea maxima culpa.* They remain bowed till they have answered *Amen* after *Misereatur vestri.* Then, kneeling erect, they make the sign of the cross at *Indulgentiam.* During the remainder of the introductory prayers they bow (bow M) toward the altar. When the priest goes up to the altar the servers rise, and without genuflecting they go to their places and kneel on the lowest step.

At the Kyrie.   At the *Kyrie* they answer *Kyrie eleison* once, *Christe eleison* twice, and again *Kyrie eleison* once. After *Dominus vobiscum,* whenever it is said, they answer *Et cum spiritu tuo,* and after *Per omnia saecula saeculorum* they say *Amen.*

During the Epistle the priest rests his hands on the Missal or on the altar. When he finishes reading it he raises his left hand slightly. Both servers answer *Deo gratias* and rise. The first steps back slightly but does not leave his place or genuflect. The second goes to the middle, genuflects, and transfers the Missal as explained in Section 29. At the beginning of the Gospel he stands on the top step and makes the triple sign of the cross with the priest. If the Holy Name of Jesus occurs at the beginning of the Gospel, he bows (bow H). He descends to the floor by the side steps, and goes to his place behind the priest. At the end of the Gospel both answer *Laus tibi Christe,* and kneel. They do not stand during the *Credo.* If the *Credo* is said, they bow (bow H) when the priest genuflects at the words *Et incarnatus est.*

At the Offertory.   When the priest removes the veil from the chalice, both servers rise, genuflect at the middle, and go to the credence table. The first takes the wine cruet, the second the water cruet.[9] They go up to the top step, and when the priest approaches they bow to him (bow H). The first hands him the wine cruet. He kisses it both before he presents it to the priest, and again on receiving it back. The second presents the water cruet in the same manner. See Section 18. Then bowing (bow H),

---

9. Callewaert, p. 167.

they turn facing each other and go to the credence table. In presenting the cruets and at the *Lavabo* bow H is made four times in all.

At the Lavabo. The first server holds the unfolded finger towel by its upper corners, the second takes the water cruet in his right hand and the basin in his left.[10] They return to the top step but stand somewhat farther to the left than when they presented the cruets. They bow to the priest when he approaches and the second server gently pours a little water over his fingers. The cruet is held about an inch above the priest's fingers. It should be held steadily and not moved about in circles. On receiving back the towel they bow and replace the cruet, dish, and towel on the credence table. The cruets are placed on the table, not on the wet dish. They now return to the front of the altar, genuflect at the middle, and kneel at their usual places. At the *Orate fratres* they wait till the priest has turned again to the altar, then kneeling erect they answer *Suscipiat Dominus,* etc.

At the Preface. The servers answer the versicles at the beginning of the Preface, and the first rings the bell three times at the *Sanctus.* See Section 24b. If the Elevation Candle is to be lit, the first server, without genuflecting, goes to the Epistle side to light it. See Section 31.

At the Elevation. At the prayer *Hanc igitur* the priest holds his hands over the chalice. The first server rings the bell. Both rise, and each approaches the middle to a point just below where he is to kneel on the platform. Without genuflecting they go up and kneel on the edge of the platform. The first kneels at the right of the priest, the second at the left. If the platform is narrow, they may kneel on the top step instead. During the Consecration the servers bow, hold the chasuble, and ring the bell, as directed in Sections 24 and 32.

---

10. Fortescue, p. 83.

After the Elevation. After the elevation of the chalice the servers rise, turn toward each other, descend to the floor, genuflect at the middle, and go to their places. They answer at the end of the *Pater Noster,* and they bow (bow H) and strike their breasts at the *Agnus Dei.* At the *Domine non sum dignus* they do not strike their breasts, but the first server rings the bell each time these words are pronounced. See Sections 9h and 24a.

If Communion Is Not Distributed. The servers bow (bow M) while the priest receives the Sacred Host. Both rise when he genuflects after removing the pall from the chalice. They do not come to the middle or genuflect. The first goes to the credence table for the cruets; the second goes to the Gospel side. They genuflect on the floor, and go up to the top step on their respective sides. They bow (bow M) while the priest receives the Precious Blood. The first ministers at the ablutions as in "Low Mass with One Server." When the first server has poured wine and water into the chalice for the second ablution, the second transfers the Missal to the Epistle side. After placing the book on the altar he descends to the floor by the side steps. Both servers then go to the front of the altar, genuflect at the middle, and go to their places. But if Communion has been distributed, and the cloth is still spread at the rail, they adjust the cloth before going to their places.

If Communion Is Distributed. When the priest removes the pall from the chalice, the servers rise, genuflect at the middle, and go to arrange the communion cloth at the rail. On returning to the altar they genuflect and go to kneel on the side steps facing each other.[11] Bowing (bow M) they say the *Confiteor.* Read Section 25.

If the Servers Communicate. The first server takes the card, paten, or plate from the credence table, and after

---

11. Menghini, p. 26.

the priest has said the *Indulgentiam* they go up and kneel
on the platform in front of the priest. After receiving Communion they go down to the floor, genuflect, and return to
their places on the side steps. If one or both of them are to
assist at the communion rail, they should observe what is
said in Section 25.

If the Clergy Communicate.   The first server takes
a communion cloth from the credence table. After the
Indulgentiam they meet at the middle, genuflect, and go
up to the top step. Each takes an end of the cloth. They
separate and kneel facing each other at opposite ends of
the platform. The cloth should be held by its four corners,
and kept reasonably tight. After the last communicant
has received, they retrace their steps. They go down to
the floor at the middle, genuflect, and kneel at their
respective places on the side steps till the tabernacle
door has been closed.

Communion of Clergy and Servers.   See Section 26,
where this matter is fully treated.

After the Ablutions.   The servers kneel in their
usual places and answer the prayers till the beginning of
the Last Gospel. They do not kneel at the middle for the
blessing.

If the Last Gospel is to be read from the Missal, the
priest will leave the book open. Immediately after
answering at the *Ite missa est* the second server transfers the Missal in the usual way. If the blessing is given
as he is passing the middle with the book, he kneels
there to receive it. Otherwise he receives it while kneeling on the lowest side step near the Missal at the Gospel
side. After the blessing he rises. He answers at the
Dominus vobiscum, etc., and goes to his place behind the
priest. At the end of the Gospel both answer *Deo gratias.*

During the Prayers after Mass.   When the priest
comes down from the platform, the servers kneel beside

him on the lowest step.[12] After the prayers, when the priest goes up to the altar to get the chalice, the first server goes for the biretta. If the Missal is to be taken back to the sacristy, the first server observes what is prescribed for the server in "Low Mass with One Server." When the priest comes down to the floor the server hands him the biretta. The servers genuflect, whether the priest bows or genuflects. They precede him to the sacristy, and again bow with him to the crucifix. The first assists him to unvest, and the second extinguishes the candles and brings the cruets to the sacristy. For the extinguishing of the candles and the care of the cruets, see Sections 10 and 19, respectively.

---

12. Wapelhorst, p. 157; Menghini, p. 23; De Carpo-Moretti, p. 203; Callewaert, p. 167.

Chapter 4

High Mass with Two Acolytes: *Missa Cantata* (Sung Mass)

THE TWO ACOLYTES in High Mass observe in general all that is prescribed for the two servers in Low Mass. The few points in which their duties differ are stated below.

Things to Be Prepared

The usual things are prepared as for a Low Mass. In addition:

a) Either four or six candles are lit on the altar.

b) The Missal is open on the bookstand.

c) The chalice may also be placed on the altar.

d) If the *Asperges* takes place, the chasuble and maniple are usually put on the bench. The *Asperges* card is placed on the altar step. In this Mass the acolytes do not carry candles.

e) If a cleric is present who is to sing the Epistle, an additional Missal is placed on the credence table.

f) If the choir or clergy are present, the acolytes bow as directed in Section 8.

The Asperges

The *Asperges* takes place before the principal Mass on Sunday, and on no other day. The acolytes assist at the blessing of the water in the sacristy and in doing so they make the following responses:

Priest: Adjutórium nostrum in nómine Dómini.
Acolytes: Qui fecit caelum et terram.
Priest: Dóminus vobíscum.
Acolytes: Et cum spíritu tuo.

They answer *Amen* at the end of each of several prayers, and also after the third cross which the priest makes with the salt which he mixes with the water.

Going to the Altar.   All bow to the cross in the sacristy and the acolytes precede the celebrant to the altar. The first acolyte carries the vessel of holy water and the sprinkler. No one takes holy water at the sacristy door. The acolytes walk abreast; the first is at all times at the right of the second.

At the Altar.   On arriving before the altar the first acolyte receives the biretta which he places temporarily on one of the steps. Both genuflect with the celebrant and kneel beside him on the lowest step.[1] The first gives him the sprinkler, and the second hands him the *Asperges* card. The celebrant sprinkles the altar, then himself, after which he rises and sprinkles the acolytes. If there are clergy present, the acolytes are sprinkled after the clergy, in which case they stand while being sprinkled.

The Sprinkling of the People.   The acolytes rise as soon as they have been sprinkled. They genuflect with the celebrant and accompany him when he goes to sprinkle the people. When leaving the altar they change sides behind the celebrant, the first passing in front of the second. The first acolyte carries the vessel of holy water, and both hold the edges of the cope. On arriving again at the

---

1. *Baltimore Ceremonial*, p. 68.

altar they genuflect. The second presents the *Asperges* card. The first acolyte puts away the holy water vessel and sprinkler, and returns immediately to his place beside the priest. After the prayer all genuflect and go to the bench where the celebrant takes off the cope and puts on the maniple and chasuble.[2] The second takes the cope to the sacristy, and the first assists the celebrant to vest. They precede the celebrant to the altar and Mass begins.

The Mass

Postures. If there is no *Asperges,* the acolytes without candles enter the sanctuary and conduct themselves during the preparatory prayers as do the two servers in Low Mass. Moreover, they kneel during the entire Mass except during the two Gospels or when performing some duty, or while the celebrant is seated at the bench.

At the Bench. At the *Gloria* or *Credo,* or whenever the celebrant is to sit down, he usually genuflects at the altar and goes directly to the bench. The acolytes promptly go to the middle, genuflect, and likewise go to the bench. But if for any reason the celebrant genuflects on the floor instead of on the platform, the acolytes genuflect with him at the middle and precede him to the bench. They arrange the chasuble over the back of the bench, and the first presents the biretta as soon as the celebrant is seated.

While the celebrant is at the bench the acolytes may either stand or sit. (a) They may stand one on each side of the celebrant, facing each other. (b) They may sit on stools placed in front of, and toward the ends of, the celebrant's bench. Before they sit down they bow (bow H) to the celebrant. They likewise bow (bow H) during the *Gloria* and *Credo* while the choir sings the words that are printed in italics in the "Prayers at Mass." During the *Credo* at the words *Et incarnatus est,* etc., if the acolytes

---

2. This may also be done in the sacristy or before the altar. S.R.C. 2027, 3; 3110, 4; 3108, 16.

are standing, they must kneel. If they are sitting, they may remain seated.[3] But if it is customary for them to kneel, they may kneel.[4] In either case they bow (bow H). At the end of the *Gloria* and *Credo,* if the acolytes are seated, they rise and bow to the celebrant. The first receives his biretta and places it on the bench. They accompany the celebrant to the altar, genuflect with him, and kneel in their usual places.

At the Gospel. The second acolyte transfers the Missal as in Low Mass. However, as soon as he has placed the book on the altar at the Gospel side, he goes to his place on the floor behind the celebrant. The choir, not the acolytes, answers the versicles at the beginning of the Gospel.

Additional Servers

Torch-Bearers. There may be torch-bearers in High Mass, who will do all that is prescribed for the torch-bearers in Solemn High Mass. They enter the sanctuary with their torches at the *Sanctus* and remain till after the Elevation, or if Communion be distributed, till after Communion.[5] If there are no torch-bearers, the acolytes themselves should not carry torches, but one of them may light the candles in the two large candlesticks which may stand either in the sanctuary in front of the altar, or one may be placed on each side of it.[6]

The Chanter of the Epistle. If the first acolyte is a cleric, he sings the Epistle. At the beginning of the last Collect he rises, goes to the credence table for the Missal, and returns to his place. At the conclusion of the Collect, at the words *Jesum Christum,* if they occur,

---

3. S.R.C. 1421, 3; 1476, 1; 1594, 2; 3860.
4. S.R.C. Sept. 17, 1897.
5. Schober, p. 170, n. 3.
6. De Herdt. I, p. 411. Whatever is here stated regarding either torch-bearers or candles is permitted but not prescribed.

he bows (bow H) toward the altar. He then goes to the middle, genuflects, and if the clergy are present he bows to them, first to those at the Gospel side, and then to those at the Epistle side. He returns to his place behind the celebrant, opens the book and sings the Epistle. At its conclusion he again goes to the middle, genuflects and bows as before, and replaces the Missal on the credence table.

The Chief Assistant. The number of servers that may be employed in High Mass is not limited by any rubric, but it would be well to bear in mind what is said in Section 23. The following passage which was inserted by Father O'Connell in his revision of Fortescue is based on decrees of the Congregation of Rites.[7]

"In addition to his functions as a server at Low Mass the chief assistant to the celebrant at a sung Mass may perform the following offices: (1) if he is a layman he may assist at the Missal (turning the leaves, etc.) and may hold the hand-candlestick for prelates who are entitled to its use; (2) if he is a cleric (i.e., initiated by the reception of tonsure) he is to sing the Epistle, and may at the Offertory carry the chalice to the altar; and after the ablutions— when it has been wiped by the priest—he may reveil it and carry it to the credence table; if he is in major orders (i.e., at least a subdeacon) he may at the Offertory wipe the chalice and pour in the wine and water; he may during the Canon remove and replace the pall whenever this is required; and after the ablutions he may wipe the chalice, reveil and remove it as he would at a Solemn Mass."[8]

---

7. S.R.C. 3377, 1, and 4181.
8. *The Roman Rite,* p. 145. Comment: The decrees do not say that a lay server may assist at the book. O'Connell, in his own work, says: "So the rubricians say, by analogy with the Low Mass of a prelate, when such assistance is allowed even to a lay server (S.R.C. 4181, 7), and in accordance with the directions given in the introduction to *Memoriale Rituum." The Celebration of Mass,* Vol. III, p. 196, 12.

Chapter 5

Requiem High Mass with Two Acolytes

A REQUIEM HIGH MASS with two acolytes differs only slightly from an ordinary High Mass with the same number of servers. The chief points of difference are:

1. The Psalm *Judica* and the *Gloria* and *Credo* are not said.

2. If the celebrant sits down during the singing of the *Kyrie* or during the *Dies Irae,* the acolytes also sit or stand as explained in "High Mass with Two Acolytes."

3. The Missal is not transferred when the celebrant has finished reading the Epistle. This is done immediately after the *Dies Irae* when the celebrant and acolytes return to the altar from the bench.

4. Neither the cruets nor any other object is kissed.

5. The breast is not struck at the *Agnus Dei.*

6. If there are torch-bearers, their candles remain lit from the *Sanctus* till after Communion.

7. If there are clergy present, they may hold lighted candles on three separate occasions: (a) during the Gospel; (b) from the *Sanctus* till after Communion; (c) during the Absolution after Mass. The second acolyte, with a taper, should attend to the lighting of the candles. He lights them for the first time toward the end of the *Dies Irae,* and again during the Preface, and finally, during the Last

Gospel, unless there is a sermon. In this case they are lit after the sermon.[1]

The Absolution

The absolution is a ceremony which frequently follows a Requiem Mass. It takes place at the casket if the body is present, and at the catafalque if the body is absent. For this ceremony it will be convenient to have a master of ceremonies, a thurifer, a server who carries the holy water, a cross-bearer, and two acolytes with lighted candles in their candlesticks.

At the end of Mass the additional servers enter the sanctuary. The celebrant assisted by the master of ceremonies takes off the chasuble and the maniple on the floor at the Epistle side, and he puts on a black cope. The servers immediately occupy positions before the altar as indicated in Figure 13. All face the altar. A genuflection is made in common. The cross-bearer and acolytes do not genuflect.

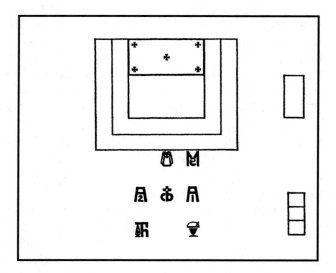

Fig. 13. Funeral: positions just before going to the casket and on returning to the altar.

---

1. See paragraph h, p. 34.

See Section 20. All turn and go toward the communion rail, the thurifer and server leading the way. These two withdraw toward the left. The cross-bearer and acolytes go around the right side of the casket and stand at the far end of it, facing the altar. If space permits they should stand at some distance from it to enable the celebrant the more easily to pass around it. The master of ceremonies carries the *Ritual* and holds the book before the priest when it is needed. He stands at the left of the celebrant, who reads or sings from the book with his hands joined. The book-bearer does not hold the book directly in front of the celebrant but stands somewhat toward his left. The thurifer and the server with the holy water likewise stand at the celebrant's left, but a little in the rear. See Figure 14.

As soon as all are in their places, the celebrant begins the ceremony of the Absolution by reading the prayer *Non intres* from the *Ritual* held open before him by the master of ceremonies. If the print is small, the priest may prefer to hold the book himself.

When the choir begins to repeat the words *Libera me Domine,* incense is put into the censer as usual. To assist at this the master of ceremonies passes to the right of the celebrant. He holds the edge of the cope with his left hand and the incense boat in his right. When incense has been put in and blessed, the thurifer with the censer and boat returns to his place. He does not swing the censer.

When the celebrant intones the *Pater Noster,* the server with the holy water presents the sprinkler to the master of ceremonies, who in turn hands it to the celebrant. Then these two genuflect toward the altar, and the celebrant goes around the casket to sprinkle it. The master of ceremonies walks at his right and holds the edge of the cope. When passing the cross the celebrant bows; the master of ceremonies genuflects. On returning to the communion rail the latter takes the sprinkler and gives it to the server. He receives the censer from the thurifer and presents it to the celebrant. The genuflection toward the altar is repeated, and the casket is incensed. The same ceremonies are observed as when it was sprinkled.

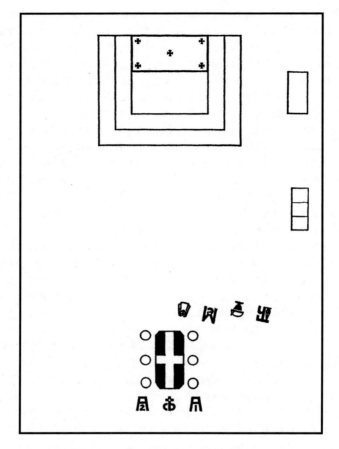

Fig. 14. Positions at the casket.

After the casket has been incensed, the censer is given back to the thurifer, and everyone resumes his original position (Fig. 14). The book-bearer holds the book before the priest, who with joined hands sings the versicles and the remaining prayers.

At the conclusion of the prayers all return to the altar before which they take their former positions (Fig. 13). They genuflect and retire to the sacristy, the thurifer and his companion leading the way. See Section 20.

Chapter 6

Solemn High Mass

Things to Be Prepared

In the Sacristy. The vestments for the celebrant, deacon, and subdeacon are laid out on the vesting table in the following order:

Subdeacon	*Celebrant*	*Deacon*
amice	amice	amice
alb	alb	alb
cincture	cincture	cincture
maniple	maniple	maniple
tunic	stole	stole
	chasuble	dalmatic

If the *Asperges* takes place, which can happen only on Sunday, the celebrant puts on a cope instead of the chasuble. In that case the chasuble and the three maniples are placed on the bench in the sanctuary.

In their proper places there will also be prepared: cassocks and surplices for the servers, the acolytes' candlesticks with lighted candles in them, the censer and incense boat, torches ready to be lit at the *Sanctus,* and if the *Asperges* takes place the holy-water vessel and sprinkler.

At the Altar. Six candles are lit, and the Missal is on the bookstand open at the Mass of the day. The three altar

cards are on the altar; and if the *Asperges* takes place, the
Asperges card is on the altar step.

On the Credence Table. Here are prepared: the
cruets, basin, and towel; a book of Epistles and Gospels or
an extra Missal properly marked; the chalice prepared for
Mass and covered with its own veil and with the humeral
veil of the subdeacon. For convenience's sake the burse is
placed on top of the humeral veil.

Postures

Below are given the general rules for standing, kneeling, and sitting to be observed by all the servers in the
sanctuary. Exceptions are either given in their proper
place or they are self-evident.

a) During the *Asperges* .... *stand.*
b) At the beginning of Mass .... *kneel.*
c) When the celebrant goes up to the altar   ... *stand.*
d) Whenever the celebrant is seated............ *sit.*
e) When the celebrant rises to go to the altar. . *stand.*
f) During the Epistle, and while the celebrant
    reads the Gospel .... *sit.*
g) During the Gospel sung by the deacon ..... *stand.*
h) While the celebrant says the *Credo*........ *stand.*
i) During the sung *Credo*[1] .... *sit.*
j) At the end of the sung *Credo* .... *stand.*
k) After *Oremus* at the Offertory.............. *sit.*
l) While being incensed.................... *stand.*
m) During the Preface .... *stand.*
n) After the *Sanctus*....................... *kneel.*
o) After the Elevation of the chalice .... *stand.*
p) After Communion........................... *sit.*
q) At *Dominus vobiscum* before
    Post-communions .... *stand.*

---

1. At *Et incarnatus est* all who are seated remain seated, but those who are standing must
kneel. S.R.C. 1421, 3; 1476, 1; 1594, 2; 3860. But a decree of Sept. 17, 1897, permits
those who are seated to kneel, where that is the custom. In either case, they bow (bow
H). On the feasts of Christmas and the Annunciation all must kneel.

r) At the blessing . . . . *kneel.*

s) During the Gospel . . . . *stand.*

t) To the above rules for kneeling and standing an important general exception must be made. On certain days all must kneel instead of stand during the Collects and Post-communions and from the *Sanctus* to the *Pax Domini sit semper vobiscum.* This applies to all Requiem Masses, and to *weekday* Masses (those said in violet vestments) of Advent, Lent, the Ember Days, and on fasting vigils. However, on account of their festive nature, this rule does not apply to the vigils of Christmas, Easter, and Pentecost; nor to Holy Thursday and the Ember Days in the week following Pentecost.

The Procession to the Altar

Thurifer

Second Acolyte   First Acolyte

Torch-bearers without torches

Master of Ceremonies

Subdeacon

Deacon

Celebrant

So far as the servers are concerned, the above order is not changed whether the *Asperges* does, or does not, take place. If the sacristy is behind the altar, the procession enters the sanctuary at the Gospel side and returns to the sacristy by the Epistle side.[2]

The Asperges. When all are vested, at a sign from the master of ceremonies, they bow to the cross in the sacristy and enter the sanctuary. The thurifer carries the vessel of holy water and the sprinkler. The acolytes carry their candlesticks as directed in Section 21. The torch-bearers observe the directions given in Section 22.

---

2. S.R.C. 3029, 12.

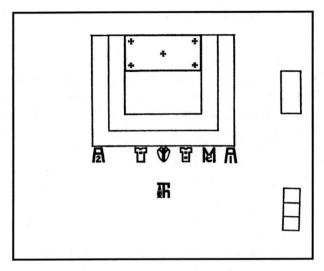

Fig. 15. Positions on arriving at the altar when the Asperges does not take place.

No one takes holy water at the sacristy door. At the genuflection before the altar all but the thurifer occupy the positions indicated in Figure 15. If there is a liturgical choir (or clergy) present, all bow in accordance with the rules given in Section 8. This Section should be studied with care.

The master of ceremonies receives from the deacon his own biretta and that of the celebrant, and he passes to the left of the subdeacon for the third. He places them on the bench and kneels at the Epistle side facing the Gospel side. The acolytes, without genuflecting again, go to the credence table and place their candles on the rear corners of it. They kneel there facing the Gospel side. The thurifer genuflects and kneels at the right of the deacon, and the torch-bearers go to their places and kneel.

All stand as soon as the deacon and subdeacon rise after the celebrant has intoned the *Asperges.* The thurifer genuflects with the celebrant and ministers and walks at the right of the deacon during the sprinkling of the people. He carries the holy-water vessel in his right hand. On returning to the altar he takes the vessel and sprinkler to the sacristy.

After the prayer the celebrant and ministers genuflect and go to the bench. The master of ceremonies assists the celebrant to remove the cope and put on the maniple and chasuble. The deacon and subdeacon put on their maniples and Mass begins.

THE MASS

The duties of each server are given separately.

The Thurifer

The censer is needed four times: (a) at the Introit; (b) at the Gospel; (c) at the Offertory; and (d) at the Elevation. On entering and leaving the sanctuary, if there are clergy present, the thurifer observes what is said in Section 8 regarding bows. His usual place in the sanctuary is between the acolytes at the credence table, upon which he places the incense boat, unless there is a boat-bearer. Whenever he goes up to the altar to have incense put in, he goes up by the side steps at the Epistle side, not by the front steps. The thurifer should be familiar with the contents of Sections 11–14.

If there is no *Asperges,* the thurifer with the censer enters the sanctuary at the head of the procession. After the genuflection which he makes behind the celebrant, he goes to his place at the credence table, where he stands facing the altar.[3]

---

3. "Or he may not come out at all till toward the end of the *Confiteor.* If he comes out at the beginning it is not clear whether he should stand or kneel during the opening prayers and confession. Some authorities say that he should kneel. Others suggest that he should stand. This seems the more convenient, since he is carrying the thurible." Fortescue, rev. ed., p. 96.

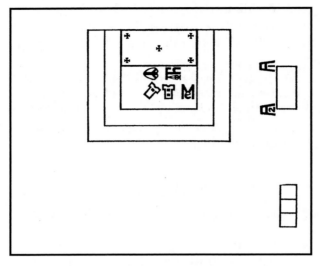

Fig. 16. Positions while incense is being put in.

At the Introit.   When the celebrant goes up to the altar the thurifer promptly ascends to the platform, and stands as indicated in Figure 16. He hands the incense boat to the master of ceremonies or to the deacon, and holds the censer open before the celebrant while incense is being put in and blessed. He closes the censer, hands it to the deacon, receives back the boat, and goes to his usual place. When the deacon goes down to the floor to incense the celebrant, the thurifer stands at his right, bowing with him before and after the incensing. He takes the censer to the sacristy, and if necessary he renews the charcoal. It is important that the censer contain glowing coals. He leaves the censer in the sacristy and returns to his place in the sanctuary.

At the Gospel.   At the end of the Epistle he goes to the sacristy for the censer. As soon as the celebrant has finished reading the Gospel, the thurifer again goes up to the platform by the side steps at the Epistle side to

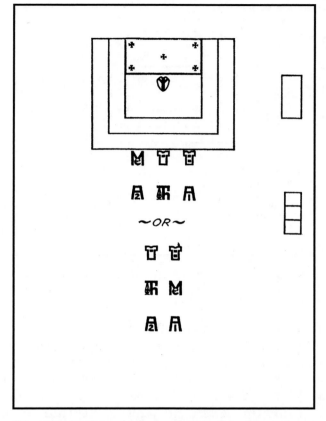

Fig. 17. Position before going to the place where the Gospel is sung.

have incense put in and blessed. He retains the censer and goes down to the floor at the Epistle side where he leaves the boat on the credence table. He precedes the acolytes to the front of the altar, and stands at some distance from the steps as indicated in Figure 17. The thurifer and acolytes do not genuflect on arriving before the middle of the altar. They wait till the deacon and subdeacon come and stand in front of them. At a sign from the master of ceremonies all genuflect and, if there are clergy present, all bow to them, bow-

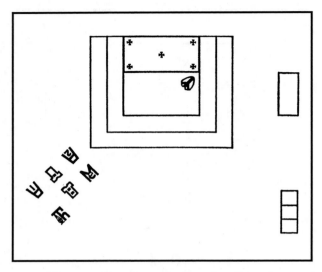

Fig. 18. Positions during the Gospel.

ing first to the Epistle side and then to the Gospel
side. The thurifer and master of ceremonies then lead
the way to the place where the Gospel is sung. The
thurifer stands at the left of the deacon, and a little
behind him as shown in Figure 18. When the deacon
sings *Sequentia sancti Evangelii,* the thurifer gives
the censer to the master of ceremonies, who in turn
presents it to the deacon. On receiving it again the
thurifer does not swing it lest its smoke annoy the
deacon. At the end of the Gospel he hands the censer
to the deacon, and stands at his right while the latter
incenses the celebrant. Both bow (bow H) to the celebrant before and after he is incensed.

On receiving the censer, if there is a sermon, the thurifer genuflects at the middle and goes to the sacristy.
But if the *Credo* is intoned, he bows with the celebrant
at the word *Deum,* genuflects, and goes to the sacristy.
If there is neither sermon nor *Credo,* he genuflects, and
goes to the credence table, for the censer will soon be
needed.

At the Offertory. Immediately after the offering of the chalice, and before the *Lavabo,* the thurifer again goes up to the platform, and everything is done as at the Introit. After the altar has been incensed, the deacon, with the thurifer at his left, incenses the celebrant, clergy, and subdeacon. Both observe the usual bows (bow H). After the deacon has incensed the subdeacon he gives the censer to the thurifer and goes to his place behind the celebrant. The thurifer, standing at the Epistle corner, incenses the deacon with two double swings. Then, in succession, he incenses with one double swing each the master of ceremonies, the first, and the second acolyte. Finally, standing at the altar rail, he incenses the people with three single swings, middle, left, and right. He now returns to the middle where the torch-bearers are awaiting him. After the usual genuflection he precedes them to the sacristy, bowing to the choir, if present, as directed in Section 8.

At the Elevation. At the *Sanctus* he again enters the sanctuary at the head of the torch-bearers, observing as before the provisions of Section 8. He goes to the Epistle side, but remains near the corner of the steps facing the Gospel side. Just before the consecration he goes to the master of ceremonies to have incense put in the censer. He then kneels on the lowest step at the right of the master of ceremonies, and incenses the Blessed Sacrament with three double swings at each Elevation. A profound bow of the head is made before and after the incensing of the Host, and again at the incensing of the chalice. In practice, a double swing is made each time the bell is rung. After the Elevation he rises, genuflects at the middle, and without bowing to anyone he goes to the sacristy. If the torch-bearers are to enter the sacristy at this time, he genuflects with them and precedes them. His duties as thurifer are now ended. He returns to the sanctuary either alone or with the torch-bearers. He genuflects and goes to his place at the credence table, where he remains standing. Where it is customary, he receives the *Pax* from the master of ceremonies, and he in turn gives it to the first acolyte. The latter gives it to the second.

Additional Duties. If the acolytes are serving as torch-bearers, the thurifer takes their place on the following occasions: (a) Toward the end of the *Pater Noster* he goes up to the platform by the side steps to remove the veil from the shoulders of the subdeacon; (b) He and the master of ceremonies hold the cloth for the Communion of the clergy; (c) He presents the cruets for the ablutions; (d) He takes the chalice veil from the credence table to the Gospel side of the altar.

When there is no master of ceremonies, the thurifer should supply his place: (a) at the bench whenever the celebrant is seated; (b) by holding the book while the altar is being incensed both at the Introit and the Offertory; (c) he accompanies the subdeacon while the latter is giving the *Pax;* (d) he attends to the birettas at the end of Mass. He should not, however, assist at the Missal.

At the Last Gospel. During the Last Gospel the thurifer leads the acolytes to the front of the altar. He does not genuflect, unless the celebrant does so during the Last Gospel. When the celebrant comes down to the floor, all genuflect and go to the sacristy in the same order in which they entered the sanctuary at the beginning of Mass.

The Acolytes

The acolytes should, as far as possible, be of the same height.[4] After vesting in cassock and surplice, one of them lights six candles on the altar and their own candles in the sacristy. They assist the deacon and subdeacon to vest.

---

4. Caer. *Ep.,* I, 2, 9.

They take their candlesticks, and at a signal from the master of ceremonies they bow to the cross with the celebrant and follow the thurifer to the altar. On entering the sanctuary, they bow to the clergy if present and form with the celebrant and his assistants a single line facing the altar.[5] See Figure 15. After the genuflection they go to the credence table, upon the rear corners of which they place their candles. They kneel there facing the Gospel side. If the *Asperges* takes place, they kneel till the deacon and subdeacon rise. The acolytes then rise and remain standing till the celebrant and ministers go to the bench. The acolytes also go to the bench. The first hands the maniple to the deacon, the second assists the subdeacon. The *Asperges* ceremony is treated in detail above on p. 73.

Mass Begins. If there is no *Asperges,* the acolytes, after the genuflection before the altar, go to the credence table, upon the rear corners of which they place their candles. No additional genuflection is made by the second acolyte while passing the middle. Their regular place during Mass, whether they stand, kneel, or sit, is at the credence table. During the introductory prayers they kneel on the floor and answer the prayers with the deacon and subdeacon. They rise when the celebrant goes up to the altar.

At the Kyrie, Gloria, etc. Whenever the celebrant and ministers go to sit down, the acolytes precede them and stand behind the bench, if that be possible. The first stands back of the deacon's seat and holds his biretta. When the deacon sits, the acolyte arranges his dalmatic in the same manner that the deacon arranged the celebrant's chasuble. He then presents the biretta. The second acolyte renders like assistance to the subdeacon. They then go to their own seat near the credence table. Should it be necessary for them to pass before the celebrant they bow (bow H) to him. For the duties of the

5. If the sanctuary is narrow, they may genuflect behind the deacon and subdeacon. The thurifer, if there is no *Asperges,* occupies a position between them.

acolytes when the deacon and subdeacon wear folded chasubles, see Section 33c.

At the Gospel.   While the celebrant, after reading the Gospel, is putting incense into the censer, the acolytes take their candlesticks.

When the thurifer comes down from the platform at the Epistle side, the acolytes follow him to the front of the altar. They do not genuflect till both the deacon and subdeacon come to stand in front of them (Fig. 17). Then at a sign from the master of ceremonies all genuflect together; and if there are clergy present, all bow first to those at the Epistle side, then to those at the Gospel side. The acolytes follow the thurifer to the place where the Gospel is sung. There they swing around, and during the singing of the Gospel the first acolyte stands at the right of the subdeacon and the second at his left. The three stand in a straight line facing in the same direction (Fig. 18). During the Gospel they do not make the sign of the cross, nor do they genuflect or bow, even though all others do so. At the end of the Gospel they immediately go to the middle, genuflect, and without bowing to anyone, they return to the credence table.

At the Credo.   The acolytes stand while the celebrant recites the *Credo,* and they genuflect with him at the words *Et incarnatus est.* When the celebrant and ministers go to the bench, the acolytes assist as at the *Kyrie* and *Gloria.* While the choir sings *Et incarnatus est . . . et homo factus est* the acolytes observe what is said under Postures i). When the deacon rises to come to the credence table for the burse, the acolytes also rise and remain standing till he returns to the bench. When the deacon goes to the altar, the acolytes go to the bench and assist the deacon and subdeacon as at the beginning of the *Credo.* Returning to their places they again sit.

At the Offertory.   When the celebrant returns to the altar and sings *Oremus,* the subdeacon comes to the

credence table for the chalice. Either the master of ceremonies or the second acolyte places the humeral veil on
his shoulders. The second acolyte receives the chalice veil
from the subdeacon and folds it. He does not go to the
altar. The first acolyte with the cruets follows the subdeacon to the altar. He presents the cruets as usual, but does
not kiss them. The acolytes remain at the credence table
while the celebrant is incensing the altar. While the deacon is incensing the celebrant the first acolyte takes the
finger towel, and the second the cruet and basin. When
the deacon is finished, both go up promptly to the top step
for the washing of the priest's hands. The usual bows are
made both before and after. They return to the credence
table and remain standing. They bow (bow H) to the thurifer both before and after he incenses them.

At the Sanctus. If the acolytes are not to act as
torch-bearers, they kneel at the credence table. One of
them rings the bell at the *Sanctus* and at other times as
in Low Mass. They kneel till after the Elevation. For
exceptions see Postures t), page 73. If they are to act as
torch-bearers, their duties will be found under "Torch-
Bearers," page 84.

At the Pater Noster. Toward the end of the *Pater
Noster* the deacon and subdeacon genuflect and go up to
the right of the celebrant. The first acolyte genuflects with
them and goes up and removes the veil from the subdeacon's shoulders. After removing the veil he goes down to
the floor, genuflects again, and places the folded veil on
the credence table.

If Communion Is Distributed. The deacon sings
or recites the *Confiteor,* and holds the paten during the
distribution of Communion. The two acolytes conduct
themselves as do the two servers in Low Mass. During
the distribution of Communion at the rail the acolytes
may accompany the celebrant with their candles. This is
permitted, not prescribed.

After Communion. At the proper time the first acolyte again takes the cruets to the altar. He genuflects on the floor before going up to the top step. He holds the cruets as at the Offertory. On receiving them again from the subdeacon he bows and returns to the credence table. The second acolyte now carries the chalice veil to the Gospel side, genuflecting as he passes the middle of the altar. He ascends by the side steps and places the veil on the altar. He retraces his steps, genuflecting again in the middle. They remain standing till the blessing.

At the Last Gospel. During the Last Gospel the acolytes follow the thurifer to the front of the altar and stand there behind him.[6] No genuflection is made unless the celebrant genuflects during the Last Gospel. When the celebrant comes down to the floor, all genuflect with him and go to the sacristy in the same order they observed on entering the sanctuary at the beginning of Mass.

The Torch-Bearers

There may be two, four, six, or eight torch-bearers, but not more. They vest in cassock and surplice as do the other servers. Their sole duty is to hold lighted torches from the *Sanctus* till the Elevation in the usual Solemn High Mass. But if Communion is distributed, and on certain other occasions, they remain in the sanctuary with their torches till after Communion.[7] It is very important that the torch-bearers should be familiar with the contents of Sections 8 and 22. And they should know when to stand, kneel, and sit as directed above under "Postures." See p. 72.

Mass Begins. At the beginning of Mass they enter the sanctuary behind the acolytes. They walk two by two,

---

6. If the procession is to move down the church the thurifer stands behind the acolytes.
7. The other occasions referred to are those listed in the second half of Postures t), page 73.

the smaller ones in front. Since they are not carrying their torches they keep their hands joined. See Section 27. After the genuflection made in common they go to their places.

At the Offertory. When the thurifer goes to incense the people, the torch-bearers form a line before the altar, leaving room for the thurifer in the middle. Or they may form two lines behind the thurifer. They genuflect with him, bow to the clergy, and follow him to the sacristy.

At the Sanctus. They again enter the sanctuary, following the thurifer. They genuflect with him, bow, and go to their places.

After the Elevation. After the elevation they genuflect and follow the thurifer to the sacristy. They put away their torches and return to their places in the sanctuary and genuflect. No bows are made to anyone on either occasion. At the end of Mass they return to the sacristy behind the acolytes.

The Acolytes as Torch-Bearers. If there are no regular torch-bearers, the acolytes supply their place. They may either use their own candles or go to the sacristy for the usual torches. They kneel at some distance in front of the altar or at the sides facing each other. If the acolytes serve as torch-bearers, the thurifer or the master of ceremonies performs the duties assigned them. It is better to have regular torch-bearers so that the acolytes may remain in their places.

The Master of Ceremonies

The duties of the master of ceremonies (M.C.) are given first in the form of a summary, then in detail. He is supposed to be familiar not only with his own duties but with the duties of everyone else in the sanctuary.

A SUMMARY

His Place. It is the duty of the M.C. to supervise and direct whatever is done in the sanctuary. For this reason the rubrics are silent regarding the place he should occupy. However, he will generally find it convenient, when not occupied with some duty, to stand at the Epistle side facing the Gospel side.

Posture. He stands throughout the Mass, kneeling only during the introductory prayers, and at the Elevation and blessing. He kneels on the lowest step.[8] If the *Credo* is said, see Postures i), page 72. He sits during the sermon, and he may either stand or sit whenever the celebrant is seated at the bench. The former is preferable.

At the Bench. During the *Gloria* and *Credo,* or whenever the celebrant is seated, the M.C. stands at the right of the deacon and slightly in front of him. He may either face the people or face in the same direction that the celebrant does.[9] At the words of the *Gloria* and *Credo,* during the singing of which the celebrant is to uncover, the M.C. first bows to him to remove his biretta and he himself inclines (bow H) toward the altar. He bows again toward the celebrant as a sign that he should again put on his biretta.

Assists at the Missal. He stands beside the celebrant and assists at the book: (a) At the Introit; (b) From the *Dominus vobiscum* after the *Gloria* till the beginning of the last Collect; (c) From the incensing of the altar at the Offertory till the *Sanctus;* (d) From the time the deacon passes to the right of the celebrant after the *Nobis quoque peccatoribus* till the *Agnus Dei* inclusive;

---

8. Schober, De Corpo.
9. Fortescue, Schober, and Van der Stappen recommend the former. Others merely direct him to stand "at the right of the deacon."

(e) From the *Dominus vobiscum* after Communion till the end of the last Postcommunion.

Whenever he is at the book he turns the pages with the hand that is farthest from the celebrant, and with the same hand, palm upward,[10] he points out passages to be read or sung.

Accompanying Subdeacon. When the M.C. accompanies the subdeacon at the Epistle and at the giving of the *Pax,* he is always at the subdeacon's left side and a little behind him.

He does not accompany the deacon to the altar after presenting him with the book before the singing of the Gospel, nor after giving him the burse during the *Credo.*

DETAILED INSTRUCTIONS

The M.C. vests in cassock and surplice. He never wears a biretta. He assists the celebrant to put on his vestments. He arranges the procession and gives a signal for all to bow to the cross in the sacristy. In the procession he walks in front of the subdeacon. At the sacristy door, if there is no *Asperges,* he offers holy water to the deacon and subdeacon, or at least to the latter. His duties during the *Asperges* have already been explained. See Figure 15.

Mass Begins. The M.C. kneels during the introductory prayers and answers with the deacon and subdeacon. At the end of the prayers he takes the boat from the thurifer, and both of them go up to the platform by the side steps, the thurifer being at his right. He presents the open incense boat to the deacon. See Section 12. When incense has been put in and blessed, he again receives the boat which he returns to the thurifer. He takes the Missal and stand and goes down to the floor at the Epistle side. When the celebrant has incensed that end of the

---

10. Or more specifically, "with his hand wholly extended and with the back part of it against the book." Van der Stappen.

altar, the M.C. replaces the book and goes down again to the floor. In neither case does he genuflect. While the deacon incenses the celebrant, the M.C. stands at the deacon's right and a little behind him. Or he may stand on the top step facing the people, his right shoulder being near the Missal.[11] He then stands at the right of the celebrant and points out the Introit.

At the Kyrie.   If the celebrant and ministers sit during the *Kyrie,* the M.C. accompanies them to the bench and stands at the right of the deacon. During the last *Kyrie* he bows to them as a sign that they should return to the altar. On arriving at the front of the altar he genuflects at the right of the deacon and goes to the Epistle side. He will observe this genuflection whenever he accompanies the celebrant from the bench to the altar.

At the Gloria.   When the celebrant intones the *Gloria,* the M.C., at the word *Deo,* directs the deacon and subdeacon by a bow to go up to the platform. He himself stands at the right of the deacon during the recitation of the *Gloria.* When it is finished he genuflects with the celebrant and leads the way to the bench, where he stands at the right of the deacon. He bows to them to remove their birettas while the choir sings *Adoramus te; Gratias agimus tibi; Jesu Christe; Suscipe deprecationem nostram;* and again *Jesu Christe.* During the singing of each of these verses he bows toward the altar. At the end of the *Gloria,* while the choir is singing *Cum Sancto Spiritu,* he bows to the celebrant as a sign that he should return to the altar. He there genuflects at the right of the deacon and goes to the Epistle side.

At the Collects.   At the *Dominus vobiscum* the M.C. goes to the Missal. He stands at the right of the celebrant and points out the Collects to be sung, and turns the pages. At the beginning of the last Collect he bows to the deacon,

---

11. Fortescue, p. 106.

who takes his place, and goes to the credence table for the book of Epistles. He holds it by the sides with both hands, with the opening toward his right. He bows but once, and that before presenting the book.[12] He then passes to the left of the subdeacon. At the end of the Collect, at the words *Jesum Christum,* if they occur, he bows to the cross, goes to the middle with the subdeacon and there genuflects with him. They bow to the clergy at the Gospel side, then to those at the Epistle side, and go to the place where the Epistle is sung. See Section 8. He stands at the left of the subdeacon while the Epistle is being sung, turning the pages if necessary. At the end of the Epistle they go to the middle, genuflect and bow as before, and go to the Epistle side. As soon as the subdeacon has received the blessing he gives the book to the M.C.

At the Gospel. As soon as the celebrant begins to read the Gospel the M.C. presents the book of Gospels to the deacon, just as he presented the book to the subdeacon. He does not accompany the deacon, but remains at the Epistle side till the celebrant has finished reading the Gospel. Incense is then put in as at the Introit. See Figure 16. He goes down to the floor at the Epistle side and leads the thurifer and acolytes to the middle of the sanctuary (Fig. 17). On arriving before the altar he does not genuflect. He stands either at the left of the subdeacon or at the right of the thurifer. Or, if he prefers, he may not join the Gospel group at all but stand to one side. When the deacon comes down from the platform with the book, all genuflect. They first bow to the clergy at the Epistle side, and then to those at the Gospel side.[13] In the procession the servers and sacred ministers proceed two by two in the following order:

Thurifer	Master of Ceremonies
Acolyte	Acolyte
Subdeacon	Deacon

---

12. Fortescue, De Herdt, Schober. Some would have him bow both before and after presenting the book.
13. Wapelhorst, Martinucci, Van der Stappen.

During the singing of the Gospel they are grouped as in Figure 18. The M.C. makes the sign of the cross when the deacon sings *Sequentia sancti Evangelii,* and taking the censer from the thurifer he hands it to the deacon. In presenting the censer he holds the chains at the top with his right hand, and near the bottom with his left. He places the upper part of the chains in the deacon's left hand and the lower in his right. When the book has been incensed he returns the censer to the thurifer. During the Gospel he stands at the right of the deacon but a little behind him. He turns the pages if necessary. If the name of Jesus occurs during the Gospel, the M.C. bows toward the book; and if the deacon genuflects, the M.C. also genuflects toward the book.[14] At the end of the Gospel he accompanies the acolytes to the middle of the sanctuary. He genuflects with them, and receives the book from the subdeacon. He bows before receiving it and places it on the credence table. If there is a sermon, he sits in any convenient place.

At the Credo. When the celebrant intones the *Credo,* the M.C., at the word *Deum,* bows to the ministers to go up to the platform. During the recitation of the *Credo* at the altar he goes up to the platform as he did at the *Gloria.* He bows, genuflects, and makes the sign of the cross with the celebrant. At the bench he conducts himself as at the *Gloria.* Bows are made at the words: *Jesum Christum; Et incarnatus est . . . et homo factus est;* and *Simul adoratur.* After bowing to the celebrant at *Et incarnatus est* the M.C. kneels. See Postures i), page 72. On rising he bows to the deacon, who accompanies him to the credence table. The M.C. there takes the burse in both hands. He holds it flat, not upright, with the open side toward the deacon. He bows, presents the burse, and

---

14. Thus Martinucci, De Carpo, Van der Stappen. Some direct the M.C. to genuflect toward the altar "as a sign to the celebrant." Others, again, as Wappelhorst and De Herdt, are silent on the subject. Fortescue would have him turn "slightly toward the celebrant." It is not easy to see why the celebrant should need a "sign" since he is looking directly at the deacon.

returns to his place. He does not accompany the deacon. At the words *Et vitam venturi saeculi* he bows to the celebrant as a sign that he should go to the altar.

At the Offertory. When the celebrant has sung *Oremus,* the M.C. bows to the subdeacon, who then comes to the credence table. He places the humeral veil over the subdeacon's shoulders, allowing it to hang down some-what lower on the right side than on the left.[15] He assists at the incensing of the altar as at the Introit. He passes over to the Gospel side and removes the Missal from the altar while the celebrant is incensing that side. He then replaces the book on the altar and remains near it till the *Sanctus*. He is incensed immediately after the deacon. He faces the thurifer, bowing with him before and after. At the last words of the Preface, *supplici confessione dicentes,* he gives a sign to the deacon and subdeacon to come to the right and left of the celebrant. He makes room for the subdeacon, who should stand next to the celebrant.[16] He bows (bow M) during the *Sanctus* and goes down to the floor with the subdeacon. He genuflects behind the subdeacon and goes to the Epistle side.

At the Elevation. Shortly before the Elevation, at *Hanc igitur,* he puts incense into the censer which is held open before him by the thurifer. He kneels on the lowest step. The bell is rung as usual. If the acolytes are acting as torch-bearers, the M.C. may attend to the bell, which is rung as in Low Mass. After the Elevation he rises and remains standing at the Epistle side till the *Nobis quoque peccatoribus*. He then goes round to the Gospel side, gen-uflecting behind the subdeacon as he passes the middle. When the deacon goes to the right of the celebrant, the M.C. takes his place at the book. On arriving at his place he genuflects with the deacon. He remains at the book till

---

15. Some authors direct the second acolyte to put the veil on the subdeacon's shoulders. Van der Stappen, Schober, Martinucci, Le Vavasseur.
16. If it is not the custom that the subdeacon goes up to the altar at the *Sanctus,* he may remain at his place on the floor. S.R.C. 2682, 30.

the *Agnus Dei,* genuflecting with the celebrant and turning the pages.

At the Pater Noster. In the preface of the *Pater Noster,* when the celebrant sings the words *audemus dicere,* the M.C., if it is necessary, makes a sign to the deacon that he should go to stand behind the celebrant. At the words *dimitte nobis* he makes a sign to the deacon and subdeacon to go up to the right of the celebrant. At the *Pax Domini* he makes room for the subdeacon at the celebrant's left. At the *Agnus Dei* he remains at the altar at the left of the subdeacon. He bows, strikes his breast at the words *miserere nobis* and *dona nobis pacem,* and, after genuflecting with the subdeacon, he goes down with him to the floor. He stands at the right of the subdeacon, but not too close. When the deacon has given the *Pax* to the subdeacon, the M.C. accompanies the latter when he gives it to the clergy.

On their return to the altar they genuflect, and the subdeacon gives the *Pax* to the M.C., and he in turn, if it is customary, gives it to the thurifer.[17] The M.C. then goes to the Epistle side, where he remains standing on the floor till the celebrant has communicated. At the *Domine non sum dignus* he does not strike his breast but bows (bow M). If Communion is distributed at the altar, he directs the acolytes to hold the communion cloth as the two servers do in Low Mass. See also Section 26.

After Communion. When the celebrant sings *Dominus vobiscum,* the M.C. goes to his right and assists at the book during the Postcommunions. At the end of the last he closes the book, unless the Last Gospel is proper to the

---

17. The *Pax* is given in all Solemn High Masses, even in those in which the Blessed Sacrament is exposed. But it is omitted in Requiem Masses, and during the last three days of Holy Week. The one who gives the *Pax* places his hands on the shoulders of the one who receives it. The latter places his hands under the arms of the one who gives it, and both incline so that the left cheek of the one almost touches the left cheek of the other. The one who gives it says, *Pax tecum;* the other answers, *Et cum spiritu tuo.* The one who gives the *Pax* bows after giving it. The one who receives it bows before and after receiving it.

day. In that case he leaves it open. The subdeacon transfers the Missal to the Gospel side.

At the blessing the M.C. kneels on the lowest step at the Epistle side. During the Last Gospel he arranges the servers in the same processional order that they had on entering the sanctuary. He takes the birettas from the bench and gives them to the deacon and subdeacon, giving the former both his own and that of the celebrant. At a sign from him all genuflect, bow to the clergy, and go to the sacristy. There they bow to the cross, and the M.C. assists the celebrant to unvest.

Chapter 7

Solemn High Mass
in the Presence of
the Blessed Sacrament Exposed

General Rules

THE FOUR GENERAL RULES given below apply to all the servers.

1. On entering and leaving the sanctuary at any time while the Blessed Sacrament is exposed, a double genuflection is made. This genuflection is made by kneeling on both knees and making a moderate inclination of both the head and shoulders. All other genuflections made during Mass are made on one knee only, and without any bow of the head.[1]

2. All bows are omitted except those made during the incensing of individuals at the Offertory. Bows made before and after incensing are regarded as a part of the act itself.

3. All kneel while the celebrant is incensing the Blessed Sacrament.[2]

4. Everyone genuflects on the floor before going up to the altar for any purpose. He genuflects again on returning to the floor.[3]

---

1. S.R.C. 2682, 49; 3426, 6; 4179, 1.
2. Schober, p. 154, Bauldry, and others.
3. S.R.C. 3975, I, 2.

The Thurifer

1. While incensing the people, the thurifer does not stand in the middle but somewhat toward the Gospel side, lest he turn his back directly to the Blessed Sacrament.

2. When the celebrant puts in incense at the Introit, Gospel, and Offertory, he does not stand directly in front of the Blessed Sacrament but somewhat toward the Gospel side. The thurifer adapts himself accordingly. He does not genuflect on the platform. See Rule 4 above.

The Acolytes

1. When making a double genuflection at the beginning and at the end of Mass, the acolytes may place their candlesticks on the floor. It is advisable for them to do so lest they incline their candles and spill wax on the floor.

2. At the *Lavabo* the celebrant stands on the second step or on the floor, facing the people. The acolytes face the celebrant and have their backs to the people.

3. It is forbidden to ring the bell at any part of the Mass even on Sundays.[4] On entering the sanctuary, the bell at the sacristy door may be gently rung.

The Torch-Bearers

1. On entering and leaving the sanctuary without torches, the torch-bearers make a double genuflection. See Section 6. But when they are carrying torches they should kneel and bow their heads only.[5]

2. In this Mass the torch-bearers do not hold lighted torches longer than in an ordinary Solemn High Mass.

3. They should be careful to observe the first three general rules given above.

---

4. S.R.C. 3157, 10 and 3448, 2. See *Matters Liturgical,* 126, and Section 24b of this book.
5. De Carpo-Moretti, p. 321.

The Master of Ceremonies

1. While all bows are omitted, this does not include such as are merely signs or invitations to others to perform some action.

2. The master of ceremonies should see that the proper number of candles are lit on the altar. This may be prescribed by the bishop of the diocese. If it is not, the following should be observed:

a) "Outside the time of the Forty Hours' Devotion, twelve, or at least ten, candles of white wax shall burn on the altar on which the Blessed Sacrament is exposed in the Ostensorium during the time of exposition."[6]

b) But during the Forty Hours' Devotion "at least twenty wax candles must burn continually on the altar."[7]

---

6. S.R.C. 3480.

7. *Matters Liturgical,* 370 and 412. The master of ceremonies should have a copy of the revised edition of the *Manual of the Forty Hours' Adoration* published by the *Amer. Eccl. Review,* or a copy of Father O'Connell's *The Clementine Instruction* (Burns, Oates, and Washbourne).

Chapter 8

Solemn High Mass
in the Presence of a Bishop
Vested in Cope

THE FOLLOWING is a brief summary of the points of difference between the usual Solemn High Mass and one at which the Ordinary assists.[1]

The bishop on entering the church prays before the altar and goes to the throne. His vestments are laid out on the altar. He vests in amice, alb, cincture, pectoral cross, stole, cope, and miter.

He is assisted by an assistant priest, two assistant deacons, a crozier-bearer, miter-bearer, book-bearer, candle-bearer, thurifer, acolytes, master of ceremonies, and others.

The Crozier-Bearer

The crozier-bearer presents the crozier directly to the bishop and receives it from him.

The bishop receives it with his left hand. See Section 17b. The bishop uses the crozier:

1. When he goes from the throne to the altar, or from the altar to the throne.

---

1. For a detailed account see Stehle's *Manual of Pontifical Ceremonies,* Fortescue's *The Roman Rite,* and the *Baltimore Ceremonial.* The first two contain diagrams.

2. While the deacon is singing the Gospel.
3. When he goes to the kneeling bench at the *Sanctus*.
4. When he returns to the throne after the Elevation.
5. At the blessing at the end of Mass.

The Miter-Bearer

Two miters are used. The precious miter is used throughout the Mass except from the *Kyrie* to the Preface, during which time the gold miter is used. The miter is put on and taken off as follows:

Put on:	*Taken off:*
1. After the cope.	1. Before the *Asperges*.
2. After the *Asperges*.	2. At the foot of the altar.
3. Before returning to the throne.	3. Before the bishop reads the Introit.
4. After the recitation of the *Kyrie,* if the bishop sits.	4. After the singing of the *Kyrie*.
5. After the recitation of the *Gloria*.	5. After the singing of the *Gloria*.
6. After the Collects.	6. After blessing the deacon before the Gospel.
7. After the recitation of the *Credo*.	7. After the singing of the *Credo*.
8. Before reading the Offertory verse.	8. At the beginning of the Preface.
9. After the recitation of the *Sanctus*.	9. On arrival at the kneeling bench.
10. After the Elevation.	10. On arrival at the throne.
11. At the ablution.	11. At *Dominus vobiscum*.
12. Before giving the blessing.[2]	12. Before the Last Gospel.
13. After the Last Gospel.	13. When unvesting.

---

2. An archbishop does not use the miter.

The Book and Candle-Bearers

The book-bearer, with the candle-bearer at his right, approaches the throne four times with the Missal:
1. For the Introit.
2. As soon as the subdeacon has sung the Epistle.
3. For the Offertory, at *Oremus.*
4. For the Communion verse.
5. For the blessing, the Canon, not the Missal, is used.

The Thurifer and Acolytes

Incense is put in at the throne at the Introit, Gospel, and Offertory. The thurifer kneels while presenting the censer; the assistant priest holds the incense boat.

1. At the Introit. After incense has been put in and blessed by the bishop, the thurifer carries the censer to the deacon at the altar. After the altar and celebrant have been incensed, he takes the censer to the assistant priest who incenses the bishop.

2. Before the Gospel. The thurifer retains the censer, and both he and the acolytes conduct themselves as they are directed to do in a Pontifical High Mass. At the end of the Gospel the censer is presented to the assistant priest.

3. At the Offertory. Everything is done as at the Introit, except that after the incensing of the altar, the deacon, not the thurifer, takes the censer to the throne. After the bishop has been incensed, the thurifer accompanies the deacon while the latter incenses the bishop's assistants and the clergy. He then incenses the deacon with two double swings, and the servers and people as usual.

Chapter 9

Solemn Requiem Mass

AS FAR AS THE SERVERS are concerned, the ceremonies of a Solemn Requiem Mass differ from those of a Solemn High Mass in the points treated below.

Postures

The rules for standing, kneeling, and sitting as given under Postures in Solemn High Mass are observed. The exceptions that occur in Solemn Requiem Mass are there given in detail. See paragraph t), page 73.

Some Things Omitted

The Psalm *Judica,* the *Gloria* and the *Credo* are omitted in Solemn Requiem Masses. The breast is not struck at the *Agnus Dei,* nor is the *Pax* given. The humeral veil is not used. There is no blessing at the end of Mass. However, the usual bows are made during the Mass.

The Thurifer

During Mass, incense is used only twice:

1. At the Offertory.   Only the altar and celebrant are incensed. The thurifer incenses no one. He leads the torch-bearers to the sacristy as usual, and returns with them at the *Sanctus.*

2. At the Elevation. The master of ceremonies puts incense into the censer. The thurifer gives the censer to the subdeacon, who incenses the Blessed Sacrament. The thurifer kneels beside him.

3. If the Absolution is given after Mass, incense will be needed a third time. The ceremonies of the Absolution are given below.

The Acolytes

1. The first acolyte lights six candles on the altar. He also lights the acolytes' candles which are carried to the altar in the usual way and remain lit on the credence table during Mass. See Section 21.

2. While the deacon is singing the Gospel the acolytes stand beside the subdeacon with their hands joined. Their lighted candles remain on the credence table.

3. At the Offertory, when the subdeacon takes to the altar the chalice with its veil and burse, both acolytes follow him. The first carries the cruets as usual. The second receives the chalice veil from the subdeacon. He folds it and places it on the credence table.

4. The acolytes assist at the washing of the priest's hands at the *Lavabo* just as they do in an ordinary Solemn High Mass. Some authorities recommend that this be done by the deacon and subdeacon.

The Master of Ceremonies

1. Immediately after the singing of both the Epistle and the Gospel the subdeacon hands the book to the master of ceremonies, for the celebrant does not bless the subdeacon after the Epistle nor does he kiss the book after the Gospel.

2. The celebrant and ministers may sit during the singing of the *Dies Irae*. They return to the altar while the choir is singing the verse *Inter oves locum praesta* (15 lines from the end).

3. During Mass the clergy may hold lighted candles:[1]

a) While the Gospel is being sung.

b) From the *Sanctus* till Communion.

c) At the Absolution after Mass, if it is given.

The master of ceremonies should appoint someone to light these candles with a taper. They should be lit toward the end of the *Dies Irae;* again during the Preface; and finally, during the Last Gospel, if the Absolution follows.

If there is a sermon, it will take place at the end of Mass, but before the Absolution. The candles would then be lit after the sermon.

The Torch-Bearers

The torch-bearers remain kneeling in the sanctuary from the *Sanctus* till Communion.[2]

The Absolution after Mass

At the end of Mass the celebrant and ministers go to the bench. The celebrant, assisted by the master of ceremonies, takes off the chasuble and the maniple and puts on a black cope. The ministers also remove their maniples. The subdeacon takes the processional cross and the acolytes their candlesticks. They go to the altar and stand before it, as shown in Figure 19. At a sign from the master of ceremonies, all but the cross-bearer and acolytes genuflect (Section 20). Then all go to the casket or catafalque. The subdeacon and the acolytes stand at the end of the casket farthest from the altar, facing the celebrant. The celebrant stands at the other end but slightly toward the Epistle side. He faces the cross. The master of ceremonies stands at his right, and the deacon at his left. The server with the holy water, and the thurifer are at the left of the deacon, but a lit-

---

1. See paragraph h), pp. 34–35.
2. *Rit. cel. Missam* VIII, 8.

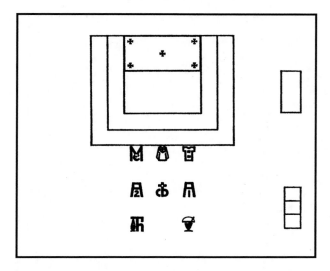

Fig. 19. Funeral: positions just before going to the casket and on returning to the altar.

tle behind him. See Figure 20. For the funeral of a priest the above positions at the head and foot of the casket are reversed.[3]

When the choir begins to sing the *Libera me Domine* a second time, incense is put in and blessed. The deacon holds the incense boat. The thurifer receives back the boat and keeps the censer.

When the celebrant intones the *Pater Noster* he receives the sprinkler from the deacon, and accompanied by the latter he goes around the casket and sprinkles it. The thurifer then gives the censer to the deacon, and the casket is incensed in the same manner that it had been sprinkled. Only the deacon accompanies the celebrant. No one else moves from his place.

---

3. The celebrant and his assistants stand at the end of the casket farthest from the altar. The cross-bearer and the acolytes are at the other end. The celebrant always stands at the foot of the casket, the cross-bearer at the head. The feet of a deceased priest are toward the people, as if in death he still faces them from the altar, as he did in life. A layman's feet, on the contrary, are always turned toward the altar which he faced in life, and now faces in death. If a priest's body is not present during the Absolution, the positions at the catafalque are the same as they would be for a layman.

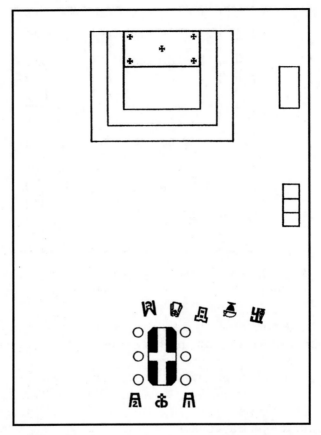

Fig. 20. Funeral: positions at the casket.

At the end of the Absolution all return to the altar, genuflect in the same order as before, and go to the sacristy.

This ceremony is treated somewhat more in detail in the Absolution following Requiem High Mass with Acolytes. It will be seen that where there is no deacon or subdeacon a server holds the cross, and the master of ceremonies takes the deacon's place. See p. 68.

Chapter 10

Pontifical High Mass

The Inferior Ministers: General Statement

ALL THE INFERIOR MINISTERS are vested in cassock and surplice. Four of these servers are called chaplains. They are the crozier-bearer, miter-bearer, book-bearer, and candle-bearer. The first two should wear humeral veils or scarfs, and all four of them, if they are clerics, may wear copes if it is customary.[1] The veils are worn under the copes. Their positions at the throne are given in Figure 21. While the bishop is at the throne the chaplains so stand that they turn their backs neither to the altar nor to the bishop.[2] Their positions at the altar at the beginning of Mass are shown in Figure 22. During the *Gloria* and *Credo* they sit on the front steps of the throne, and the other servers on the side steps of the altar. Before sitting they put away the crozier, miter, book, and candle.[3] Or, they may stand in their regular places during the *Gloria* and *Credo*. More specific instructions as to the positions of the inferior ministers must be obtained from the master of ceremonies who will take into account the size and shape of the sanctuary.[4]

---

1. *Caer. Ep.* Lib. I, XI, 1.
2. Schober, p. 297.
3. Schober, Fortescue, De Herdt, and others.
4. See the numerous diagrams or figures in Stehle, Fortescue, Schober, and in the later editions of Wapelhorst. Their diagrams agree except in matters of minor importance.

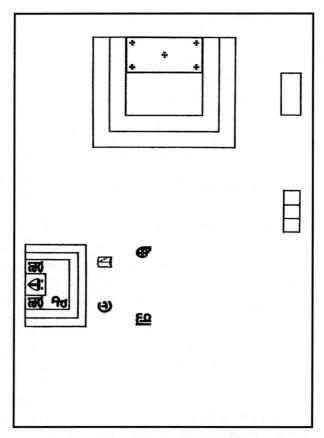

Fig. 21. Positions at the throne.

The *Ceremonial of Bishops* directs ministers in pontifical functions to genuflect to the bishop of the diocese as often as they approach him, depart from him, or pass before him.[5] But, "In the United States a custom prevails of making a profound bow, instead of a genuflection, to the Ordinary officiating or assisting at Mass, Vespers, or other functions."[6] "A custom of forty years' standing may dispense from a positive law of the Church, according to

5. *Caer. Ep.* I, XVIII, 3.
6. Stehle, p. 293.

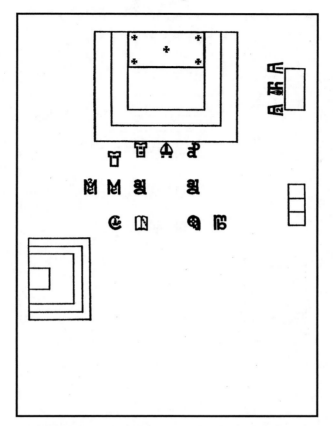

Fig. 22. Positions at the altar at the
beginning of Mass.

canon 27, 1, of the Code of Canon Law [1917 Code].
Wapelhorst is right therefore in affirming that in this
country, on account of a long custom, it is not necessary
to genuflect to the bishop of the diocese in the course of a
Pontifical High Mass. A deep bow is sufficient."[7]

The *Asperges* does not take place before a Pontifical
High Mass.

---

7. *Amer. Eccl. Review,* Dec., 1932, p. 643. Fortescue plainly disapproves of such genuflections.
   The Roman Rite, p. XXIII.

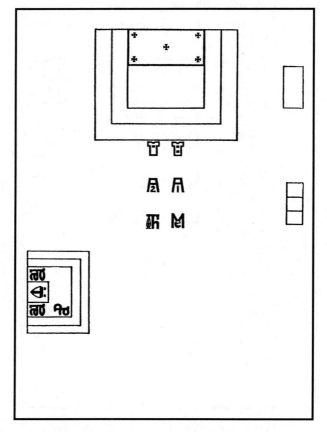

Fig. 23. The Gospel group before the altar.

The Crozier-Bearer

GENERAL RULES

1. The crozier-bearer holds the crozier in his right hand, with the crook turned toward the people. The sleeve of the surplice, or the humeral veil if he wears one, is held between his hand and the crozier. While walking he raises the crozier from the ground. He carries it with both hands and with the crook facing forward.

2. The crozier-bearer himself gives the crozier to the bishop and receives it directly from him. He gives it into

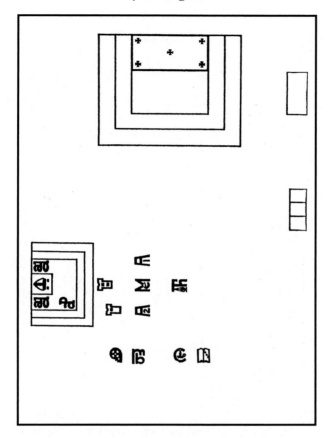

Fig. 24. The Gospel group at the throne.

the bishop's left hand, and in doing so he observes the usual kisses. See Section 17b.

3. In presenting the crozier he hands it to the bishop with the crook turned toward himself.

4. In processions, when the crozier-bearer carries the crozier, he walks in front of the bishop; but when the bishop carries the crozier the crozier-bearer walks behind him.

5. In general, the bishop uses the crozier: (a) whenever he goes from the throne to the altar, or from the altar to the throne; (b) while the deacon is singing the Gospel; (c) at the blessing at the end of Mass.

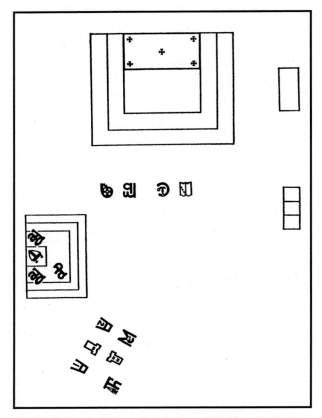

Fig. 25. The Gospel group while the Gospel
is being sung.

PARTICULAR INSTRUCTIONS

When the bishop is vested he sits and receives the
miter. The crozier-bearer goes to the throne. The bishop
rises, receives the crozier, and goes to the altar. The
crozier-bearer follows him and receives the crozier at the
foot of the altar before the miter is removed. He returns
to his place.

The bishop incenses the altar, after which he is
incensed at the Epistle side. The crozier-bearer then goes
up to the platform, presents the crozier, and follows the
bishop to the throne, where he again receives it.

At the Gospel the crozier is presented to the bishop when the deacon sings *Dominus vobiscum.* After the Gospel it is received from the bishop before he kisses the book.

After washing his hands at the Offertory, the bishop rises and goes again to the altar. The crozier is presented and received as at the beginning of Mass.

At the end of Mass the crozier-bearer presents the crozier for the blessing at the words *omnipotens Deus,* and receives it immediately after the blessing. If the Last Gospel is that of St. John, the bishop merely begins it at the altar; he then takes the crozier and goes to the throne, reciting the Last Gospel on the way. The crozier-bearer should, therefore, remain near the bishop. But if the Last Gospel is proper, he goes to his place after the blessing; and at the end of the Last Gospel he will go up to the platform and present the crozier. He follows the bishop to the throne and there receives it.

The Miter-Bearer

GENERAL RULES

1. The miter-bearer wears a humeral veil, with the ends of which he covers his hands. He holds the miter with the bands or lappets turned toward himself. Only one miter is held at a time. The other is placed on the altar at the Epistle side, or on the credence table. No miter should rest on the altar after the Offertory.

2. The two miters are used as follows: (a) The precious miter is used until the Introit, during the reading of which the miter is not used; (b) The golden miter is used from the Introit till the end of the sung *Credo;* (c) The precious miter is then used till the end of Mass.

3. It is important for the miter-bearer to know to whom he should present the miter. At the throne it is given to the deacon who is at the bishop's right, and it is received from the one at his left. At the altar, with two exceptions, he presents it to the deacon of the Mass. As in Solemn High Mass, the altar is incensed before the Introit and at the Offertory. The deacon incenses the bishop at the Epistle

side. On these two occasions the miter is presented to the first assistant deacon who puts it on the bishop.

4. In general, the bishop wears the miter:

(a) whenever he goes from the throne to the altar, or from the altar to the throne; (b) while being incensed, or while washing his hands; (c) when seated while the choir sings anything; (d) while the subdeacon sings the Epistle; (e) while he reads the Epistle and Gospel, seated on the throne; (f) while giving the blessing. In this instance an archbishop does not use the miter. Note the application of the above general rules in the particular instructions below.

PARTICULAR INSTRUCTIONS

Miter is put on:	*Miter is taken off:*
1. At Terce, after the cope.	1. At the *Dominus vobiscum* before the Prayer.
2. After the chasuble.	2. At the foot of the altar.
3. At the altar, after incensing it.	3. On arrival at the throne.
4. If the bishop sits after reciting the *Kyrie*.	4. At the end of the *Kyrie* sung by the choir.
5. When the bishop sits after reciting the *Gloria*.	5. At the end of the *Gloria* sung by the choir.
6. When the bishop sits after singing the Collects.	6. After blessing the deacon before the Gospel.
7. When the bishop sits after reciting the *Credo*.	7. At the end of the *Credo* sung by the choir.
8. After Oremus and the Offertory verse.	8. At the foot of the altar.
9. At the altar, after incensing it.	9. At the *Lavabo,* before the *Gloria Patri* following it.
10. After the second ablution; it is put on at the Epistle side.	10. After the bishop has washed his hands.
11. At the blessing, before *Sit nomen Domini.*	11. Immediately after the blessing.
12. When the bishop is about to leave the altar.	12. On arrival at the throne.

The Book-Bearer

GENERAL RULES

1. When the bishop sings anything from the book, it is held by the assistant priest; but when he reads from the book, it is held by the book-bearer. At the Offertory, when the bishop sings *Oremus* and reads the Offertory, the book-bearer, not the assistant priest, holds the Missal. He holds the book with the back of it resting against his forehead, and with both hands he supports it from below. The height at which the book is held should be carefully judged.

2. When the bishop reads standing, the book-bearer stands. When the bishop reads sitting, the book-bearer kneels on the top step of the throne.

3. While holding the book he does not bow or genuflect, nor does the candle-bearer, whose companion he is.

4. As a rule, the book is held directly in front of the bishop. But while the bishop is washing his hands or vesting, the book-bearer stands slightly to the left of the bishop.

5. When not required for use the book need not be held. When carrying the book it should be closed. It is carried as shown in Section 28.

6. It is important that the book-bearer knows which book, Canon or Missal, to present, and when to present it. This information follows. But it will help greatly if he bears in mind that the Missal is used only for those parts of the Mass which are proper. At other times the Canon is used. The propers said at the throne are: the Introit, Collects, Epistle, Gospel, and Offertory; and at the altar, the Communion verse and the Postcommunions.

PARTICULAR INSTRUCTIONS

The Canon and Missal are used:

1. CANON, at the throne while the bishop is vesting.

2. MISSAL, for the Introit, which the bishop reads standing at the throne after incensing the altar.

3. CANON, for the *Gloria*. The assistant priest holds it while the bishop sings the opening words. The book-bearer holds it while he reads the remainder.

4. MISSAL, for the Collects; held by the assistant priest.

5. MISSAL, for the Epistle, Gradual, and Gospel, which the bishop reads after the subdeacon has sung the Epistle and kissed the bishop's ring.

6. CANON, for the *Credo*. The same as at the *Gloria*.

7. MISSAL, at the end of the sung *Credo*. It is held by the book-bearer while the bishop sings *Dominus vobis-cum* and *Oremus* and reads the Offertory verse.[8] After the bishop has washed his hands, the assistant priest carries the Missal and stand to the altar, or he may direct the book-bearer to do this. At the altar the assistant priest attends to the books.

8. CANON, for the thanksgiving after Mass.

The Candle-Bearer
GENERAL RULES

1. Candle, Book.   The candle-bearer holds the candle in his right hand. He assists at the book both at the throne and at the altar. While holding it he never bows or genuflects, nor does his companion, the book-bearer.

2. At the Throne.   His position is at the left of the book-bearer. He stands when the book-bearer stands, and kneels when he kneels. When not required for use, the candle need not be held. It may be placed near the book or in some other becoming place, but not on the altar.

3. At the Altar.   His place from the Offertory till Communion is at the left of the assistant priest. During the Elevation he leaves the candle on the altar and kneels on the lowest step. After Communion his place is at the book on the Epistle side.

---

8. So Stehle, Schober, and Wapelhorst. But Martinucci and Fortescue would have the assistant priest hold the book during the sung words.

4. With the Book-Bearer. The candle-bearer should be familiar with the duties of the book-bearer, whose companion he is. They regularly come and go, stand or kneel, bow or genuflect, together.

The Thurifer

The duties of the thurifer are practically the same as those of the thurifer in Solemn High Mass. The following points are deserving of special attention:

1. In general, his place is at the credence table. He ministers the censer kneeling. At the altar, he hands the incense boat to the deacon; at the throne, to the assistant priest.

2. At the Introit and at the Offertory incense is put in and blessed at the altar as usual, except that the thurifer kneels.

3. After the Epistle, when the deacon has kissed the bishop's ring, the thurifer goes to the throne to have incense put in for the Gospel. On approaching the throne he bows to the bishop and kneels on the step of the throne. He gives the boat to the assistant priest. After the incense has been put in and blessed he rises, bows, and goes to form a part of the Gospel group as in Solemn High Mass. The thurifer, followed by the acolytes, leads the procession from the altar to the throne, and from the throne to the place where the Gospel is sung. See the Figures illustrating the positions of the Gospel group at the altar, at the blessing, and during the Gospel. The thurifer should read what is prescribed for the acolytes at the Gospel.

After the Gospel the thurifer hands the censer to the assistant priest and holds his cope while the latter incenses the bishop.

4. At the Offertory, when the deacon incenses the bishop and others in the sanctuary, the thurifer accompanies him as in Solemn High Mass. On receiving the censer he incenses the deacon with two double swings, the master of ceremonies and inferior ministers with one

double swing each, and finally the people. He leads the torch-bearers to the sacristy and returns with them at the *Sanctus.*

5. At the Elevation everything is done as in Solemn High Mass.

The Acolytes

The duties of the acolytes are practically the same as those prescribed for the acolytes in a Solemn High Mass. Their special attention is called to the ceremonies at the washing of the bishop's hands, and at the Gospel.

1. At the Washing of Hands. The acolytes kneel while assisting at the washing of the bishop's hands. The assistant priest presents the towel to the bishop. He washes his hands four times in all, the first two times at the throne, the last two at the altar:

a) Before vesting.
b) After reading the Offertory verse.
c) At the *Lavabo,* after the bishop has been incensed.
d) After the second ablution.

2. At the Gospel. When the thurifer goes to the throne, the acolytes with their candlesticks go to the front of the altar as in Solemn High Mass. When the Gospel group is in place, all genuflect and go to the throne where they kneel till the deacon has received the blessing. Then, bowing to the bishop, they go to the place where the Gospel is sung. See the figures illustrating the positions.

3. At Terce. The acolytes may have an additional duty to perform if Terce is sung while the bishop is putting on his vestments. At a sign from the master of ceremonies they take their candles and go to the bishop's seat. They bow to him and stand facing each other before the lowest step while the bishop sings the prayer from the book held open before him by the assistant priest.

After the prayer they bow and return to their place. This ceremony takes place in the *secretarium,* a chapel where Terce is sung and the bishop vests.

The Gremial-Bearer

1. The gremial-bearer carries the gremial folded before his breast, but he presents and receives it open. It is carried with both hands.

2. His position from the Introit till the Offertory is at the throne. The gremial is presented to the first assistant deacon after he has put the miter on the bishop. It is received from the second assistant deacon before he takes off the miter.

3. It is placed on the bishop's knees while he sits:

a) After reciting the *Kyrie* (if he sits).

b) After reciting the *Gloria.*

c) While the subdeacon sings the Epistle. It is not removed till the bishop has blessed the deacon before the Gospel.

d) During the sermon.

e) After reciting the *Credo.*

f) After *Oremus* at the Offertory. The bishop sits and washes his hands. He then goes to the altar, and the gremial is no longer used. It is folded and placed on the credence table.

The Train-Bearer

Whenever the bishop walks, the train-bearer follows him and holds the train at its extreme end, and in such a way that it does not touch the floor.

When the bishop kneels, the train-bearer kneels at the end of the train and allows it to rest on the floor.

When the bishop sits, the train-bearer extends the train, or arranges it as best he can.

---

9. *Caer. Ep.* Lib. I, Cap. XV, 1.

At the throne, his place is on the floor at the left of the bishop. During the *Gloria* and *Credo* he sits on the lowest side step of the throne at the left of the bishop. There should be only one train-bearer.[9]

The Torch-Bearers

The torch-bearers do all that is prescribed for the torch-bearers in Solemn High Mass. In addition they do what is prescribed below for the Clerks of the Vestments. There should not be more than eight torch-bearers.[10]

The Clerks of the Vestments

It is advisable that there should not be too much ceremony or pomp about the conveying of the vestments from the altar to the throne. At a signal from the second master of ceremonies the clerks approach the altar, genuflect, and bow to the bishop. The first in rank goes up to the second step, receives the amice, genuflects, and goes immediately to the throne. He bows to the bishop, and gives the amice to the first master of ceremonies. In like manner, the second in rank receives the alb, the third the cincture, and so on. After presenting a vestment, each one bows to the bishop, genuflects before the altar, and returns to his place. This is one method of carrying out the ceremony of vesting the bishop. At the end of Mass, when the bishop takes off the vestments, they may be carried back to the altar in a similar manner.

---

10. *Caer. Ep.* Lib. II, Cap. VIII, 68.

Chapter 11

Vespers

General Directions

VESPERS MAY BE CELEBRATED with varying degrees of solemnity. Three of these methods are here described under the following headings:

1. Simple Vespers.
2. Solemn Vespers.
3. Pontifical Vespers.

Simple Vespers is another name for Vespers in which the celebrant is assisted by servers only, by two acolytes, a thurifer, and, if possible, by a master of ceremonies. There are no assistants in copes.

Solemn Vespers is the name given to the same Office when the celebrant is assisted by two, four, or even by six assistants vested in copes, and by the same number of servers that are employed in Simple Vespers.

Pontifical Vespers are celebrated by a bishop or by some other prelate enjoying the use of pontifical vestments and insignia.

Simple and Solemn Vespers do not differ greatly. Simple Vespers are treated first, and the duties of each server are given with considerable detail. They are given with less detail in Solemn and in Pontifical Vespers. It is presumed that the servers in the more solemn functions are familiar with their corresponding duties in Simple Vespers.

Vesture. In Vespers, whether Simple, Solemn, or Pontifical, the servers vest in cassock and surplice. In addition, the crosier-bearer and the miter-bearer in Pontifical Vespers wear humeral veils or scarfs, and if they are clerics, they may wear copes.

Candles. Six candles are lit on the altar. In Simple and Solemn Vespers the acolytes' candles are lit in the sacristy, but they are extinguished as soon as the acolytes arrive at the altar. In Pontifical Vespers they are first lit after the *Magnificat.*

During Vespers the acolytes' candlesticks rest on the lowest side step or on the floor, one at each side of the altar. The candles in them are extinguished,[1] and the thurifer, sacristan, or one of the acolytes relights them during the last psalm.

The Sign of the Cross, Bows. All make the sign of the cross at *Deus in adjutorium meum intende,* and at the beginning of the *Magnificat.*

All bow as often as the choir sings the *Gloria Patri,* and at the doxology (last stanza) of the hymn. They also bow at the names of Jesus, Mary, or of the saint whose feast is celebrated or commemorated. Where it is customary, a bow may be made at the verse *Sanctum et terribile nomen ejus* (Ps. 110), and at *Sit nomen Domini benedictum* (Ps. 112).

Postures during Vespers

If there is a liturgical choir (if the clergy in the sanctuary sing the Office), the servers stand, kneel, and sit as the members of the choir stand, kneel, or sit. Any exceptions to this rule are either self-evident or they are given in the proper place. If there is no liturgical choir, the

---

1. This is the plain prescription of the *Caer. Ep.* Lib. II, Cap. III, n. 2. The new De Carpo-Moretti (1932) gives the rule, as do all authorities, but adds: "The custom of not extinguishing the candles may be retained" (p. 47). The rule, not the custom, should be observed.

servers, unless otherwise directed, observe the rules given below, which the celebrant also observes.[2]

Kneel.   During the prayer *Aperi, Domine,* which is said on arriving at the altar. Rise when the celebrant rises.

Sit.   When the first psalm has been intoned (at the asterisk of the first verse). They sit during the psalms and antiphons, but stand for the intonation of the antiphon.

Stand.   When the celebrant rises to sing the Chapter. All stand till the end of Vespers. They sit, however, while the choir sings the antiphon after the *Magnificat,* and before it also, if it is sung entire. The antiphon before the *Magnificat* is often merely intoned.

Kneel.   During the first stanza of the hymns *Veni Creator Spiritus* and *Ave maris stella,* and during the stanza *Tantum ergo* of the *Pange lingua,* if the Blessed Sacrament is exposed on the altar; but if it is in the tabernacle, all stand or kneel according to the custom of each church.[3] They kneel also during the stanza *O crux ave spes unica* of the hymn *Vexilla regis.*

Bows to the Choir.   The usual bows are made. These are explained in Section 8.

---

2. The following books are recommended for the servers and laity: *The Layfolks Vesperal,* containing the complete text, in Latin and English, of the Offices of Vespers and Compline for every day in the year, with Litanies, Hymns, and Devotions for Benediction. Also a pamphlet, *The Offices of Vespers and Compline for Sundays.* And for Benedictine churches, *The Benedictine Vesperal,* Latin and English text. All of the above are published by Burns, Oates and Washbourne, London. The Catholic Truth Society publishes a pamphlet, *Vespers for Sunday,* with notes by Fortescue.
3. S.R.C. 1280, 2.

Chapter 12

Simple Vespers

ALL THE SERVERS should be familiar with the General Directions given in the preceding section.

The Master of Ceremonies

The master of ceremonies (M.C.), assists the celebrant to vest. At a sign from him all bow to the cross. The acolytes with lighted candles lead the procession. The M.C., with the thurifer at his left, follows; then the celebrant. Holy water is taken at the sacristy door as usual.

At the Altar. On arriving at the altar the M.C. receives the celebrant's biretta, genuflects with him, and kneels on the lowest step at his right during the prayer *Aperi, Domine,* which is said silently. After the prayer they rise, genuflect, and if they are to go to the regular bench at the Epistle side, they bow first to that part of the choir which is at the Gospel side, and then to the Epistle side. "They bow to the choir on either side, first to the side opposite the place to which they will now go."[1]

---

1. Fortescue, p. 216. The reason for Fortescue's indefinite rule is obvious. The celebrant need not occupy the bench at the Epistle side. He may occupy the first stall in choir on either side. *Caer. Ep.* Lib. II. Cap. III, 4. Fortescue, p. 213. Martinucci, Vol. 1, Cap. XIV, 57. See Section 8d of this book.

At the Bench. The M.C. stands at the celebrant's right and says with him the *Pater* and *Ave.* He holds the edge of the cope while the celebrant makes the sign of the cross at the *Deus in adjutorium meum intende* and later at the *Magnificat.* When the celebrant sits, the M.C. hands him his biretta. During the psalms he sits on a stool at the right of the celebrant. Just before the *Gloria Patri* or similar words requiring a bow, he rises and bows to the celebrant as a sign that he should remove his biretta. While the choir sings these words, the M.C. bows toward the altar; then, bowing again to the celebrant, he sits down. Toward the end of the last psalm he sees to it that the thurifer or someone else relights the acolytes' candles. After the last antiphon all rise. The celebrant hands his biretta to the M.C., and rising he sings the Chapter and intones the hymn.

The Magnificat. The celebrant intones the antiphon of the *Magnificat,* and if it be doubled (sung through), he sits and resumes his biretta. The M.C. and all others likewise sit. If it is not doubled, no one sits. As soon as the cantors begin to intone the *Magnificat* all rise and make the sign of the cross. The celebrant and M.C. go to the altar, bow to the choir, genuflect, and go up to the platform. The M.C. stands at the celebrant's right as the deacon does in Mass. With his left hand he holds the edge of the cope, and with his right the incense boat. As he hands the spoon to the celebrant he says *Benedicite, Pater reverende.*

When the incense has been blessed, the M.C. gives back the boat to the thurifer and receives from him the censer which he presents to the celebrant, observing what is said in Section 13b. During the incensing of the altar he accompanies the celebrant and holds the right edge of the cope. The altar is incensed as at the Introit in Mass. When it is finished he receives the censer from the celebrant at the Epistle corner and hands it to the thurifer. The M.C. accompanies the celebrant to the middle, bows with him to the cross, goes down to the floor, genuflects, bows to the choir, and goes to the bench with him.

On arriving at the bench he takes the censer from the thurifer and incenses the celebrant with three double swings, bowing before and after. He gives the censer back to the thurifer and returns to his place at the right of the celebrant. He is incensed after the clergy.

After the Magnificat. After the *Sicut erat,* at the end of the *Magnificat,* all sit during the antiphon. When it is finished the M.C. receives the celebrant's biretta. All rise and the celebrant sings *Dominus vobiscum* and the Collect of the Office. The commemorations follow, if there are any. During the anthem of the Blessed Virgin all stand on Saturdays, Sundays, and on all days during the Paschal season. On other days they kneel, and after the anthem the celebrant alone rises to sing the prayer. Then all genuflect and go to the sacristy. They bow to the cross, and the M.C. assists the celebrant to unvest.

If Benediction follows immediately after Vespers, the celebrant and servers do not leave the sanctuary.

The Thurifer

Preparation. The thurifer prepares the fire in the censer so that it will be ready when wanted. After bowing to the cross in the sacristy he enters the sanctuary behind the acolytes and at the left of the master of ceremonies. On arriving at the altar he genuflects behind the celebrant, who kneels to say the prayer *Aperi, Domine*. He remains standing till the acolytes come to stand one on each side of him. They genuflect together and go at once to their place at the credence table or to the place assigned them. There they kneel. They rise when the celebrant rises.

During the Psalms. The thurifer sits after the intonation of the first psalm. Toward the end of the last psalm he rises and relights the acolytes' candles.[2] He

---

2. Bauldry, Falice and others recommend that the thurifer relight the candles. He can do this on the way to the sacristy.

then goes to the sacristy to prepare the censer. When the antiphon of the *Magnificat* is intoned, or a little before, he reenters the sanctuary, genuflects, and goes to the Epistle side, where he stands facing the Gospel side.

At the Magnificat. When the celebrant and master of ceremonies go up to the platform by the front steps, the thurifer goes up by the side steps. He gives the incense boat to the master of ceremonies, and incense is put in and blessed as in Mass. He gives the censer to the master of ceremonies, and receives from him the boat which he places on the credence table. He returns immediately to the platform and holds the left edge of the cope while the celebrant incenses the altar. At the Epistle side he passes to the right of the master of ceremonies from whom he receives the censer. He goes down to the floor by the side steps, turns toward his left, and goes to the bench. See Section 30. He hands the censer to the master of ceremonies and stands at his left while the latter incenses the celebrant.

The Thurifer Incenses the Clergy, etc. See Section 14. The thurifer incenses the clergy, the master of ceremonies, the acolytes, and the people as they are incensed in Mass. The clergy are incensed as follows: The thurifer bows once to all the clergy on the Gospel side, or to the side of greater dignity, and incenses each person with one double swing of the censer, then bows again. He turns, genuflects at the middle, and goes to incense in the same way those at the Epistle side.[3] At the *Gloria Patri* of the *Magnificat* he stops incensing and bows toward the altar. No one is to be incensed after the celebrant has sung *Dominus vobiscum* before the Collect. The thurifer's duties are now finished. He genuflects before the altar, and after putting away the censer he returns to his place in the sanctuary. But if Benediction follows, he remains

---

3. Fortescue, p. 124.

in the sacristy till the celebrant goes to the altar. He then enters the sanctuary at the head of the torch-bearers and assists as usual.

The Acolytes

Preparation. The first acolyte lights either four or six candles on the altar, according to the solemnity; and he lights the acolytes' candles in the sacristy. At a sign from the master of ceremonies they bow to the cross in the sacristy and head the procession to the altar. As in Mass, the first acolyte goes to the end of the front step at the Epistle side, and the second acolyte to a similar position at the Gospel side. When the celebrant arrives at the middle they genuflect with him. They go immediately to the sides of the altar and place their candles on the lowest side step, one on each side, and extinguish them. They then go to the front of the altar where the thurifer stands waiting for them. They genuflect with him and go to their place at the credence table, or to the place assigned them. They kneel while the celebrant is saying the prayer *Aperi, Domine.*

During the Psalms. See "Postures during Vespers" on page 120. They bow during the *Gloria Patri,* but the master of ceremonies alone rises and stands while it is sung. During the last psalm their candles are relit by the thurifer, or by the sacristan, or by the first acolyte.

The Chapter. After the *Gloria Patri* of the last psalm they go to the sides of the altar for their candles. They genuflect at the middle, approach the celebrant, and bow to him. Then separating, they stand facing each other, one at each side of the celebrant and slightly in front of him. See Figure 26 (on page 129). They remain in

---

4. If the hymn is the *Ave maris stella* or the *Veni Creator Spiritus,* the acolytes do not kneel even though all others do. They remain before the celebrant till he rises, then bowing to him they depart.

this position while he sings the Chapter, and till he intones the hymn.[4] Then coming together in front of him, they bow, go to the middle, genuflect, and replace their candles on the altar steps. They do not extinguish them. They should not be placed where they will be in the way during the incensing of the altar. Each acolyte, with hands joined, remains beside his candlestick till the end of the *Magnificat*. See Figure 27 (on page 130).

After the Magnificat. At the *Sicut erat* following the *Magnificat,* they again take their candles and stand before the celebrant while he sings the Collect and the commemorations, if there are any. They observe the same ceremonies as at the singing of the Chapter. When the celebrant has sung *Dominus vobiscum* the second time, they bow to him, return to the altar, and place their candles on the lowest step. They remain beside them till the end of Vespers. The procession returns to the sacristy in the same order that it entered the sanctuary.

If Benediction follows, the acolytes light the candles on the altar during the anthem of the Blessed Virgin.

Chapter 13

Solemn Vespers

IT IS PRESUMED THAT the servers are familiar with the ceremonies of Simple Vespers and with the "General Directions" on page 119 for Vespers of every kind. As far as the servers are concerned, the ceremonies of Solemn Vespers do not differ greatly from those of Simple Vespers. Only the points of difference between the two are given here.

In Solemn Vespers the celebrant is assisted by two, four, or six assistants, or clerics vested in copes. Two of these usually sit beside the celebrant at the bench, and they assist him during the incensing of the altar. The first assistant is at his right, the second at his left.

The Master of Ceremonies

At the bench the master of ceremonies takes his place at the right of the first assistant. He accompanies the first assistant when he comes before the celebrant to pre-intone the first antiphon, the hymn, and the antiphon of the *Magnificat*. And he accompanies the cantors when they go to pre-intone the antiphons to the persons of highest rank or seniority in the choir.

When the celebrant and assistants go to the altar to incense it, the master of ceremonies and the thurifer genuflect with them and go up to the platform by the side steps at the Epistle side. Incense is put in, and the altar

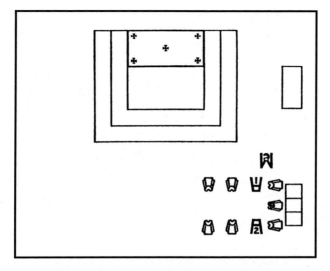

Fig. 26. Positions during the Chapter
and the Collect.

is incensed as at the Introit in Mass. The assistants take
the place of the deacon and sub-deacon. The celebrant is
incensed at the bench by the first assistant. The master
of ceremonies does not incense anyone, nor does he touch
the censer. He is incensed after the assistants.

The Thurifer

Incense is put in and blessed as at the Introit in Mass.
Two assistants in copes assist the celebrant while he
incenses the altar. The thurifer stands on the floor. He
receives the censer as usual at the Epistle side and goes
to the bench. He there gives the censer to the first assistant and stands at his right holding the edge of the cope
while the celebrant is being incensed.

If there are only two assistants or cope-bearers, the
thurifer incenses the clergy, the assistants, the master of
ceremonies, the acolytes, and the people. Each assistant
is incensed with two double swings; the others as in Simple
Vespers. But if there are four or six assistants, the first

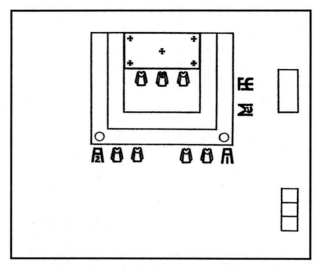

Fig. 27. Positions during the incensing of the
altar: drawing shows six assistants in copes.

incenses the celebrant, and the last (the fourth or sixth)
accompanied by the thurifer who holds the edge of his
cope, incenses the clergy and the remaining assistants.
The thurifer then receives the censer and incenses the
last assistant, the master of ceremonies, the acolytes, and
the people.

The Acolytes

The duties of the acolytes are the same as in Simple
Vespers. However, when there are four or six assistants
in copes some or all of these will also stand before the
celebrant during the Chapter and the Collect.[1] See
Figure 26. The acolytes should genuflect with them, bow
with them, and conform to them in every way, that the
greatest uniformity of action may be obtained.

---

1. See the diagrams in Schober, p. 346; Wapelhorst, p. 315; and that in Fortescue, p. 222,
   which is somewhat different.

Chapter 14

Pontifical Vespers

THE INFERIOR MINISTERS, whose duties are here outlined, vest in cassock and surplice. In addition, the crozier-bearer and miter-bearer wear humeral veils or scarfs of silk. If they are clerics, they may wear copes over their veils. The ministers of the crozier, miter, book, and candle have much the same functions as in Pontifical High Mass. They will there find explained the proper manner of holding or presenting the crozier, miter, etc. They observe the usual genuflections before the altar; and on approaching the throne and before leaving it, they bow to the bishop. See the second paragraph of the General Statement on "Pontifical High Mass," page 106.

The Crozier-Bearer

The five General Rules for the guidance of the crozier-bearer in Pontifical High Mass are equally applicable in Pontifical Vespers. These rules need not be repeated here. See page 108.

In Vespers the bishop uses the crozier:

1. At the Magnificat. When the *Magnificat* is intoned, the Bishop rises and makes the sign of the cross. The crozier-bearer presents the crozier and follows the bishop to the altar. He receives it again from the bishop at the foot of the altar before the miter is removed.

2. After incensing. When the bishop has finished incensing the altar, he receives first the miter and then the crozier on the platform at the Epistle corner. He goes to the throne and holds the crozier till the *Sicut erat* at the end of the *Magnificat.*

3. At the Blessing. This follows the *Benedicamus Domino.* The crozier is presented at the words *Omnipotens Deus,* and if Benediction follows, the bishop retains the crozier and goes to the foot of the altar, where the crozier-bearer again receives it. If the position of the throne is such that it cannot be seen by the faithful, the bishop may give the blessing from the altar.

The Miter-Bearer

Two miters are used in Vespers. The bishop uses the golden miter while he sits during the singing of the psalms. At other times, if any miter is worn, it is the precious miter. The miter which is not in use is placed on the altar at the Epistle side, with the lappets extending toward the front.

Both at the throne and at the altar the first assistant deacon is at the bishop's right, the second is at his left. The former puts the miter on the bishop, the latter takes it off. The miter is presented and received accordingly.

Miter is put on:	*Miter is taken off:*
1. After the cope, in vesting.	1. It is worn but for a moment, then taken off and placed on the altar. The golden miter is brought to the throne.
2. When the bishop sits after the first psalm has been intoned.	2. When the bishop sits after the subdeacon has sung the Chapter. The miter is not worn during the hymn.

3. When the bishop sits after intoning the antiphon of the *Magnificat.*

3. When the bishop arrives at the foot of the altar.

4. At the Epistle corner, on the platform, after the bishop has incensed the altar.

4. When the bishop sits after being incensed at the throne.

5. At the *Sicut erat* following the *Magnificat.*

5. At the end of the antiphon of the *Magnificat.*

6. For the blessing which follows the *Benedicamus Domino.*

6. If Benediction follows, the miter is taken off at the foot of the altar.

7. After Benediction, at the foot of the altar.

7. On arrival at the throne.

The Book-Bearer

The book-bearer does not hold the book before the bishop. This is done by the assistant priest. The book-bearer's duty is to present the book open to the assistant priest for the *Deus in adjutorium meum intende,* for the intonation of the first antiphon, the hymn, the antiphon of the *Magnificat,* and for the Collect and the blessing.

When not required for use for a considerable interval, the book need not be held, but may be placed on the credence table.

The Candle-Bearer

The assistant priest holds the book before the bishop. The candle-bearer stands at his left and holds the candle in his right hand. At other times he accompanies the book-bearer whose companion he is. He attends with the candle when the bishop sings *Deus in adjutorium meum intende,* and when he intones the first antiphon, the hymn, and the antiphon of the *Magnificat,* when he sings the Collect, and at the blessing following the *Benedicamus Domino.*

When not required for use the candle need not be held. It may be placed on the credence table or beside the book.

The Thurifer

When the bishop intones the antiphon of the *Magnificat* the thurifer goes to the throne, bows to the bishop, and kneels on the step. He hands the incense boat to the assistant priest and holds the censer open before the bishop. When incense has been put in and blessed he closes the censer, rises, receives the boat, bows to the bishop, and goes to the Epistle side, genuflecting as he passes the middle. He goes up to the platform by the side steps, gives the censer to the assistant priest, and goes down again to the floor. After the altar has been incensed he receives the censer at the Epistle corner. He goes to the throne and presents the censer to the assistant priest. He holds the right edge of the cope while the latter incenses the bishop.

The thurifer then gives the censer to the subdeacon or to the one who pre-intones the antiphons. The subdeacon with the thurifer at his left incenses the sacred ministers and the clergy. The thurifer receives the censer and incenses the subdeacon with two double swings. Then in order he incenses the master of ceremonies, the bearers of the crozier, miter, book, and candle, the acolytes, and the people, as in Solemn Vespers. When the bishop sings *Dominus vobiscum* before the Collect, all incensing ceases.

The Acolytes

1. The first acolyte lights six candles on the altar. The acolytes' candlesticks with unlit candles in them are placed on the altar steps before Vespers.[1]

---

1. Thus Stehle and De Herdt. But Martinucci, Fortescue, and the *Baltimore Ceremonial* would have the candlesticks placed on the credence table.

2. The acolytes do not light their candles during the last psalm, nor do they go to the throne for the singing of the Chapter. This is sung by the subdeacon, and the acolytes remain at their place at the credence table.

3. When the bishop has intoned the antiphon of the *Magnificat,* the acolytes genuflect before the middle of the altar and bow to the bishop. They then go, one to each side of the altar, and fold back the dust cloth, leaving uncovered the front half of the uppermost altar cloth.[2] Every altar is covered with three linen cloths. These in turn are covered by a dust cloth or altar cover of some colored material. It is the dust cloth, not the altar cloth, that is to be turned back. This may also be done by the sacristan before Vespers.[3] While the bishop is incensing the altar they stand facing each other, one at each side of the altar. After the incensing they replace the dust cloth. This cloth is removed before Benediction.

4. After the *Gloria Patri* of the *Magnificat* the acolytes light their candles, genuflect before the altar, and go to the throne. They bow to the bishop, and stand facing each other below the lowest step until the bishop has sung *Dominus vobiscum* the second time. Then bowing again to the bishop, they return to the altar, genuflect, and replace their candles on the altar steps, or on the credence table, if they had been kept there during Vespers. In either case, if Benediction follows, the candles are placed on the credence table.

---

2. *Caer. Ep.* Lib. II, I, 13 and 15.
3. De Herdt II, 27.

Chapter 15

Vespers in the Presence of the Blessed Sacrament Exposed

TWO CASES ARE POSSIBLE. The Blessed Sacrament has either been exposed before Vespers, or it has not. If it has already been exposed, as during the Octave of Corpus Christi, the servers enter the sanctuary as for any other Vespers. However, they make a double genuflection as explained below. Neither the censer nor lighted torches are required.

But if the Blessed Sacrament has not been exposed, the servers enter the sanctuary in the following order: the thurifer with the censer, the acolytes, at least two torch-bearers with lighted torches, the master of ceremonies, etc. The celebrant exposes and incenses the Blessed Sacrament. He then recites the prayer *Aperi, Domine* and goes to the bench. The thurifer and torch-bearers make a double genuflection and go to the sacristy to put away the censer and the torches. They return to their place in the sanctuary, again making a double genuflection. During Vespers the censer is used as usual, and the torches will be required for Benediction. The following general rules apply to all:

1. On entering or leaving the sanctuary at any time while the Blessed Sacrament is exposed, a double genuflection is made. This genuflection is made by kneeling on both knees and making a moderate inclination of both the head and shoulders. All other genuflections made

during Vespers are made on one knee only, and without any bow of the head.[1]

2. The acolytes place their candles on the side steps of the altar as usual, but they do not extinguish them.

3. All bows are omitted except those that precede or follow the incensing of anyone.

4. All kneel while the celebrant is incensing the Blessed Sacrament.[2] After putting in incense at the *Magnificat*, the celebrant kneels on the second step and incenses the Blessed Sacrament. In Simple Vespers the master of ceremonies and the thurifer kneel beside him and hold the edges of his cope.

5. A server genuflects on the floor before going up to the platform for any purpose. He genuflects again on returning to the floor.[3]

6. While incensing the people, the thurifer does not stand in the middle but somewhat toward the Gospel side, lest he turn his back directly to the Blessed Sacrament.

1. S.R.C. 2682, 49; 3426, 6; 4179, 1.
2. De Carpo-Moretti, p. 57.
3. S.R.C. 3975, I, 2.

Chapter 16

Vespers for the Dead

1. Six candles of unbleached wax are lit on the altar.

2. In Vespers for the Dead, no incense is used. Therefore, no thurifer is required.

3. In Simple and Solemn Vespers the acolytes have no duties. They lead the procession to the sanctuary carrying lighted candles of unbleached wax. They place them on the steps and extinguish them; nor do they afterwards touch them.

After the *Requiescant in pace* "the acolytes make a genuflection, and with their hands joined, they go to the sacristy, followed by the clergy and the celebrant."[1]

In Pontifical Vespers for the Dead, when the bishop sits while the antiphon of the *Magnificat* is being repeated, the acolytes with lighted candles of unbleached wax go before the bishop as usual. They remain standing though all others kneel. After the *Requiescant in pace* they bow, and replace their candles on the steps.

---

1. *Baltimore Ceremonial,* 7th ed., p. 210; see also De Carpo-Moretti, pp. 60–62.

Chapter 17

Benediction of the Blessed Sacrament with Servers Only

Introductory

IN BENEDICTION various combinations are possible. The celebrant may be assisted by servers only; he may be accompanied by a priest who will expose the Blessed Sacrament for him; he may be assisted by a deacon and subdeacon—Solemn Benediction; Benediction may be given by a bishop or by another prelate—Pontifical Benediction; the Blessed Sacrament may be exposed on a different altar from that on which it is reserved.

"Since Benediction is not a strictly liturgical service, there are, naturally, considerable local differences in its forms in different countries."[1] Most approved authors state with considerable detail the duties of the celebrant in Benediction, but they scarcely mention the servers, and where they do, their directions are both scant and vague.[2]

The number of servers is not prescribed. There must, however, be a thurifer; there should be two, four, six, or eight torch-bearers; there may be two acolytes and there may be a master of ceremonies. If there are two acolytes, the master of ceremonies might be dispensed with, and if

---

1. Fortescue, p. 255; Callewaert, p. 262.
2. Wapelhorst affords a fair example of what is meant by "scant and vague." See 10th ed., pp. 289 and 294.

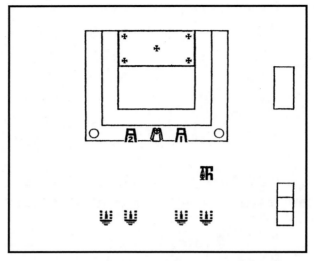

Fig. 28. Benediction with servers only.

there is a master of ceremonies, he and the thurifer can easily do what is prescribed for the acolytes.

Some General Rules

1. During Benediction all genuflections are made on one knee only.[3] But if a server enters or leaves the sanctuary while the Blessed Sacrament is exposed, he makes a double genuflection on arriving at the altar and before leaving it.[4]

2. All bow (bow M) during the singing of the words *Veneremur cernui,* which mean, "Bowing, let us adore."

3. All bow their heads profoundly when the celebrant pronounces the name of Jesus in the Divine Praises, and during the *Gloria Patri,* if it be sung after Benediction.

4. All regularly kneel unless the performance of some duty requires them to stand. At the end of Benediction they stand as soon as the Blessed Sacrament has been replaced in the tabernacle and the door closed.

---

3. S.R.C. 4179, III, 5.
4. S.R.C. 937, 6; 2682, 47; 4048, 11.

The Thurifer

Incense is put into the censer twice:[5] (1) as soon as the Blessed Sacrament has been exposed; (2) at the beginning of the stanza *Genitori Genitoque*. The same ceremonies are observed on both occasions.

The thurifer kneels during Benediction except when the performance of some duty requires him to stand. His place is behind the celebrant, between the torch-bearers. Or better still, he may kneel in front of the altar, but somewhat toward the Epistle side.

As in Mass, the thurifer stands directly in front of the celebrant while incense is being put into the censer. He hands the incense boat to whoever is standing at the celebrant's right. To him also he gives the censer as soon as incense has been put in. In presenting the censer he holds the top of the chains in his right hand. While the celebrant is incensing the Blessed Sacrament the thurifer kneels behind him. But if there is no second acolyte, he kneels at the celebrant's left and holds the edge of the cope while the Blessed Sacrament is being incensed. In either case he bows when the celebrant does. See Sections 12–13.

While the celebrant is giving the blessing with the Sacred Host, the thurifer may, where it is customary, incense the Blessed Sacrament with three double swings.[6]

The Acolytes

After the genuflection in front of the altar, the acolytes place their candles on the lowest step or on the floor.[7] They then kneel on the lowest step, one at each side of the celebrant. "Nothing," says Fortescue, "is said in any document about acolytes with their candles; it is supposed that only torch-bearers attend. However, the assistance of acolytes is not forbidden. It does not seem

---

5. Incense is put in only once if there are no special prayers or hymns between the hymn of exposition and the *Tantum Ergo*. S.R.C. 4202, 1. The celebrant, not the thurifer, is the judge.
6. This custom is permitted, but it is not prescribed. S.R.C. 3108, 6.
7. Callewaert, p. 271.

unlawful that, besides the torch-bearers behind the celebrant, also acolytes should kneel, with their candles, at his side, particularly if the number of torches possessed by the church is limited."[8]

As soon as the Blessed Sacrament has been placed in the monstrance, the second acolyte, if necessary, carries to the platform the steps by which the throne of exposition is reached. He remains kneeling on the platform till the Blessed Sacrament has been placed on the throne. He then replaces the steps on the floor. Both acolytes bow (bow M) with the celebrant and stand while incense is being put into the censer. The first holds the incense boat, the second holds the edge of the celebrant's cope. When incense has been put in, the first receives the censer from the thurifer. Both kneel beside the celebrant. The first presents the censer, and in doing so he holds the top of the chains in his right hand and the lower part in his left. He swings his right arm around gracefully in front of the celebrant to enable him to receive the censer with ease. Both acolytes hold the edges of the cope, and both bow their heads profoundly with the celebrant before and after he incenses the Blessed Sacrament. They bow (bow M) while the choir sings the words *Veneremur cernui.* At the words *Genitori Genitoque* incense is put in a second time with the usual ceremonies.

The first acolyte gets the prayer card, and at the word *Oremus* all bow their heads profoundly with the celebrant. The first acolyte, without genuflecting, goes for the humeral veil, and returning, he places it on the celebrant's shoulders as soon as he kneels.[9] The second acolyte again carries the steps to the platform if necessary. When the celebrant has placed the monstrance on the altar, the steps are removed to the floor below, and the acolyte returns to his place. During the blessing the first acolyte may ring the little bell, if it be

8. *The Roman Rite,* p. 257. Thus too Schober, p. 220.
9. S.R.C. 4179, 2.

customary. The ringing of the bell is not prescribed,[10] but where it is done it should be rung softly, gently, and not violently.

After the blessing the celebrant genuflects and goes down to his place. The first acolyte hands him the prayer card containing the Divine Praises. He removes the veil from the celebrant's shoulders, and folding it, he replaces it on the credence table.

In Solemn Benediction the deacon and subdeacon kneel beside the celebrant. It would be well to have a master of ceremonies; and if there are acolytes, they may place their candles at the ends of the lowest front step and kneel on the floor before them.

The Torch-Bearers

There should be at least two torch-bearers. "There may be four, six, or eight."[11] They enter the sanctuary with lighted torches, and observe what is said in Section 22.

---

10. *Baltimore Ceremonial,* p. 83.
11. Fortescue, p. 257.

Chapter 18

Manner of Serving a Low Mass Celebrated by a Dominican

ONLY THE POINTS OF difference between the Roman Rite and the Dominican Rite are given here. It is presumed that the server is familiar with the ceremonies of Low Mass according to the Roman Rite.

The Ceremonies

On arriving at the altar the server genuflects with the priest and immediately goes to the credence table. Wine and water are put into the chalice at the beginning of Mass instead of at the Offertory. The cruets are presented in the usual manner. However, in presenting the water cruet, except in Requiem Masses, the server says, *Benedicite*. The priest blesses the water saying, *In nomine ✝ Patris, et Filii, et Spiritus Sancti.* The server answers, *Amen.* He replaces the cruets on the credence table and goes to his place at the Gospel side.

During the *Confiteor* the server does not strike his breast at the words *mea culpa*. He does not answer *Deo gratias* at the end of the Epistle, nor *Laus tibi, Christe* after the Gospel. Nor does he make any response at the *Orate fratres.*

No water or wine is served at the Offertory, but the *Lavabo* or washing of the priest's fingers takes place after the Gospel or *Credo* in the usual manner.

After ringing the bell at the *Sanctus* the server lights the Elevation candle. See Section 31. The priest does not spread his hands over the chalice, but the server rings the bell just before the Consecration when he sees the priest making the five signs of the cross over the chalice. The bell is rung at the Elevation as usual. It is also rung three times at the *Agnus Dei,* once each time the words are pronounced. The *Domine non sum dignus* does not occur in the Mass proper, but it is said as usual just before the distribution of Communion. See Section 24a.

A server with a lighted candle accompanies the priest during the distribution of Communion. His place is at the right of the priest.

At the end of the Last Gospel the server answers *Deo gratias.*

Prayers at the Foot of the Altar

Priest: In nómine Patris, ✠ et Fílii, et Spíritus Sancti. Amen. Confitémini Dómino quóniam bonus.

Server: Quóniam in saéculum misericórdia ejus.

Priest: Confiteor, etc. (The priest says the *Confiteor.*)

Server: Misereátur tui omnípotens Deus, et dimíttat tibi ómnia peccáta tua: líberet te ab omni malo, salvet, et confírmet in omni ópere bono, et perdúcat te ad vitam aetérnam.

Priest: Amen.

Server: Confíteor Deo omnipoténti, et beátae Maríae semper Vírgini, et beáto Domínico Patri nostro, et ómnibus Sanctis, et tibi, pater: quia peccávi nimis cogitatióne, locutióne, ópere, et omissióne, mea culpa: Precor te oráre pro me.

Priest: Misereátur vestri omnípotens Deus, et dimíttat vobis ómnia peccáta vestra: líberet vos ab omni malo, salvet, et confírmet in omni ópere bono, et perdúcat vos ad vitam aetérnam.

Server: Amen.
Priest: Adjutórium nostrum in nómine Dómini.
Server: Qui fecit caelum et terram.

The priest goes up to the altar.

Reference List

Augustine, C., *Liturgical Law* (Herder, 1932).

Caeremoniale Episcoporum, latest revision, 1886. Published by Pustet, Dessain, Marietti, and others. Despite its name and poor arrangement it contains much authoritative information on ceremonies in general.

Ceremonial for the Use of Catholic Churches in the United States (The Baltimore Ceremonial), 9th ed. (Philadelphia: Kilner, 1926).

Fortescue-O'Connell, *The Ceremonies of the Roman Rite Described,* 4th ed. (London: Burns, Oates and Washbourne, 1932). An excellent work, especially in its revised form.

De Carpo-Moretti, *Caeremoniale* (Italy: Marietti, Turini, 1932).

De Herdt, J. B., *Sacrae Liturgiae Praxis,* 3 vols., 10th ed. (Louvain: Van Linthout, 1903).

De Herdt, J. B., *Praxis Pontificalis,* 3 vols. (Louvain, 1904). This is an exposition of the *Caeremoniale Episcoporum.*

Kunz, Ch., *Die Liturgischen Verrichtungen des Celebrantem;. . . der Leviten und Assistenten; . . . der Ministranten,* 3 vols. (Pustet, 1901–1904).

Le Vavasseur-Haegy, *Manuel de Liturgie et Cérémonial selon le rit romain,* 2 vols., 14th ed. (Paris; Lecoffre [Gabalda], 1928).

Le Vavasseur-Haegy, *Les Fonctiones Pontificales selon le rit romain,* 3rd ed. (Paris: Lecoffre [Gabalda], 1904).

Martinucci-Menghini, *Manuale Sacrarum Caeremoniarum,* 4 vols. (Pustet, 1911–1916).

Memoriale Rituum, translated into English by Father Clark. In it are found the ceremonies of Candlemas Day, Ash

Wednesday, and Holy Week as carried out in small churches without deacon and subdeacon (London: Burns, Oates and Washbourne, 1926).

Schober, Geo., *Caeremoniae Missarum Solemnium et Pontificalium* (Pustet, 1909). This work also contains a good treatise on the *Missa Cantata*, Solemn Vespers, Benediction, etc.

Stehle, A., *Manual of Pontifical Ceremonies,* rev. ed. (Latrobe, Pa.: Archabbey Press, 1916).

Van der Stappen, J. F., *Liturgiae Sacrae,* 3rd ed., 5 vols. (Dessain: Mechlin, 1911–1915).

Wapelhorst-Bruegge, *Compendium Sacrae Liturgiae,* 10th ed. (Benziger, 1925).

Wuest-Mullaney, *Matters Liturgical,* 3rd ed. (Pustet, 1931).

Index

TAN · BOOKS

TAN Books was founded in 1967 to preserve the spiritual, intellectual and liturgical traditions of the Catholic Church. At a critical moment in history TAN kept alive the great classics of the Faith and drew many to the Church. In 2008 TAN was acquired by Saint Benedict Press. Today TAN continues its mission to a new generation of readers.

From its earliest days TAN has published a range of booklets that teach and defend the Faith. Through partnerships with organizations, apostolates, and mission-minded individuals, well over 10 million TAN booklets have been distributed.

More recently, TAN has expanded its publishing with the launch of Catholic calendars and daily planners—as well as Bibles, fiction, and multimedia products through its sister imprints Catholic Courses (CatholicCourses.com) and Saint Benedict Press (SaintBenedictPress.com).

Today TAN publishes over 500 titles in the areas of theology, prayer, devotions, doctrine, Church history, and the lives of the saints. TAN books are published in multiple languages and found throughout the world in schools, parishes, bookstores and homes.

For a free catalog, visit us online at
TANBooks.com

Or call us toll-free at
(800) 437-5876